THE PHILOSOPHY OF CIVILIZATION

PART I

The Dale Memorial Lectures, 1922.

THE DECAY

AND

THE RESTORATION

OF

CIVILIZATION

THE PHILOSOPHY OF CIVILIZATION

PART I

BY

ALBERT SCHWEITZER

D.THEOL.; D.PHIL.; D.MED. (STRASSBURG)

TRANSLATED BY

C. T. CAMPION

M.A. (OXON.)
(SOMETIME OF MERTON COLLEGE, OXFORD)

A. & C. BLACK, LTD.

4, 5 & 6 SOHO SQUARE, LONDON, W. 1

1923

Printed in Great Britain by
THE WHITEFRIARS PRESS, LTD., LONDON AND TONBRIDGE.

To

ANNIE FISCHER

IN

DEEPEST GRATITUDE

AUTHOR'S PREFACE

" THE Decay and the Restoration of Civilization " is the first part of a complete philosophy of
civilization with which I have been occupied since
the year 1900.

The second part, entitled " Civilization and
Ethics ", will appear immediately. The third is
called " The World-View * of Reverence for Life ".
The fourth has to do with the civilized State.

That over which I have toiled since 1900 has been
finally ripened in the stillness of the primeval forest
of Equatorial Africa. There, during the years
1914–17, the clear and definite lines of this philosophy of civilization have been developed.

The first part, " The Decay and the Restoration
of Civilization ", is a kind of introduction to the
philosophy of civilization. It states the problem of
civilization.

Entering on the question as to what is the real
essential nature of civilization, I come to the pro-
nouncement that this is ultimately ethical. I know
that in thus stating the problem as a moral one I

* *Weltanschauung*. Translated 'theory of the universe' throughout
the first part and elsewhere in this preface.

shall surprise and even disgust the spirit of our times, which is accustomed to move amidst æsthetic, historical and material considerations. I imagine, however, that I am myself enough of an artist and also of an historian to be able to comprehend the æsthetic and historical elements in civilization, and that, as a modern physician and surgeon, I am sufficiently modern to appreciate the glamour of the technical and material attainments of our age.

Notwithstanding this, I have come to the conviction that the æsthetic and the historical elements, and the magnificent extension of our material knowledge and power, do not themselves form the essence of civilization, but that this depends on the mental disposition of the individuals and nations who exist in the world. All other things are merely accompanying circumstances of civilization, which have nothing to do with its real essence.

Creative, artistic, intellectual, and material attainments can only show their full and true effects when the continued existence and development of civilization have been secured by founding civilization itself on a mental disposition which is truly ethical. It is only in his struggle to become ethical that man comes to possess real value as a personality; it is only under the influence of ethical convictions that the various relations of human society are formed in such a way that individuals and peoples can develop in an ideal manner. If the ethical foundation is lacking, then civilization collapses, even when in other directions creative and intellectual forces of the strongest nature are at work.

This moral conception of civilization, which makes me almost a stranger amidst the intellectual life of my time, I express clearly and unhesitatingly, in order to arouse amongst my contemporaries reflection as to what civilization really is. We shall not succeed in re-establishing our civilization on an enduring basis until we rid ourselves completely of the superficial concept of civilization which now holds us in thrall, and give ourselves up again to the ethical view which obtained in the eighteenth century.

The second point which I desire should obtain currency is that of the connection between civilization and our theory of the universe. At the present time no regard is paid to this connection. In fact, the period in which we are living altogether misses the significance of having a theory of the universe. It is the common conviction nowadays, of educated and uneducated alike, that humanity will progress quite satisfactorily without any theory of the universe at all.

The real fact is that all human progress depends on progress in its theory of the universe, whilst, conversely, decadence is conditioned by a similar decadence in this theory. Our loss of real civilization is due to our lack of a theory of the universe.

Only as we again succeed in attaining a strong and worthy theory of the universe, and find in it strong and worthy convictions, shall we again become capable of producing a new civilization. It is this apparently abstract and paradoxical truth of which I proclaim myself the champion.

Civilization, put quite simply, consists in our giving ourselves, as human beings, to the effort to attain the perfecting of the human race and the actualization of progress of every sort in the circumstances of humanity and of the objective world. This mental attitude, however, involves a double predisposition : firstly, we must be prepared to act affirmatively toward the world and life ; secondly, we must become ethical.

Only when we are able to attribute a real meaning to the world and to life shall we be able also to give ourselves to such action as will produce results of real value. As long as we look on our existence in the world as meaningless, there is no point whatever in desiring to effect anything in the world. We become workers for that universal spiritual and material progress which we call civilization only in so far as we affirm that the world and life possess some sort of meaning, or, which is the same thing, only in so far as we think optimistically.

Civilization originates when men become inspired by a strong and clear determination to attain progress, and consecrate themselves, as a result of this determination, to the service of life and of the world. It is only in ethics that we can find the driving force for such action, transcending, as it does, the limits of our own existence.

Nothing of real value in the world is ever accomplished without enthusiasm and self-sacrifice.

But it is impossible to convince men of the truth of world- and life-affirmation and of the real value of ethics by mere declamation. The affirmative and ethical mentality which characterizes these beliefs must originate in man himself as the result of an inner spiritual relation to the world. Only then will they accompany him as strong, clear, and constant convictions, and condition his every thought and action.

To put it in another way: world- and life-affirmation must be the products of thought about the world and life. Only as the majority of individuals attain to this result of thought and continue under its influence will a true and enduring civilization make progress in the world. Should the mental disposition towards world- and life-affirmation and towards ethics begin to wane, or become dim and obscured, we shall be incapable of working for true civilization, nay, more, we shall be unable even to form a correct concept of what such civilization ought to be.

And this is the fate which has befallen us. We are bereft of any theory of the universe. Therefore, instead of being inspired by a profound and powerful spirit of affirmation of the world and of life, we allow ourselves, both as individuals and as nations, to be driven hither and thither by a type of such affirmation which is both confused and superficial. Instead of adopting a determined ethical attitude, we exist in an atmosphere of mere ethical phrases or declare ourselves ethical sceptics.

How is it that we have got into this state of lacking a theory of the universe ? It is because hitherto the world- and life-affirming and ethical theory of the universe had no convincing and permanent foundation in thought. We thought again and again that we had found such a basis for it ; but it lost power again and again without our being aware that it was doing so, until, finally, we have been obliged, for more than a generation past, to resign ourselves more and more to a complete lack of any world-theory at all.

Thus, in this introductory part of my work, I proclaim two truths and conclude with a great note of interrogation. The truths are the following : The basic ethical character of civilization, and the connection between civilization and our theories of

the universe. The question with which I conclude
is this : Is it at all possible to find a real and permanent foundation in thought for a theory of the
universe which shall be both ethical and affirmative
of the world and of life ?

The future of civilization depends on our over-
coming the meaninglessness and hopelessness which
characterize the thoughts and convictions of men
to-day, and reaching a state of fresh hope and fresh
determination. We shall be capable of this, however, only when the majority of individuals discover for themselves both an ethic and a profound
and steadfast attitude of world- and life-affirmation,
in a theory of the universe at once convincing and
based on reflection.

Without such a general spiritual experience there
is no possibility of holding our world back from the
ruin and disintegration towards which it is being
hastened. It is our duty then to rouse ourselves to
fresh reflection about the world and life.

In "Civilization and Ethics", the second part of
this philosophy of civilization, I describe the road
along which thought has led me to world- and life-
affirmation and to ethics. The root-idea of my
theory of the universe is that my relation to my
own being and to the objective world is determined
by reverence for life. This reverence for life is given
as an element of my will-to-live, and becomes clearly

conscious of itself as I reflect about my life and about the world. In the mental attitude of reverence for life which should characterize my contact with all forms of life, both ethics and world- and life-affirmation are involved. It is not any kind of insight into the essential nature of the world which determines my relation to my own existence and to the existence which I encounter in the world, but rather only and solely my own will-to-live which has developed the power of reflection about itself and the world.

The theory of the universe characterized by reverence for life is a type of mysticism arrived at by self-consistent thought when persisted in to its ultimate conclusion. Surrendering himself to the guidance of this mysticism, man finds a meaning for his life in that he strives to accomplish his own spiritual and ethical self-fulfilment, and, simultaneously and in the same act, helps forward all the processes of spiritual and material progress which have to be actualized in the world.

I do not know how many, or how few, will allow themselves to be persuaded to travel with me on the road indicated above. What I desire above all things—and this is the crux of the whole affair—is that we should all recognize fully that our present entire lack of any theory of the universe is the ultimate source of all the catastrophes and misery of our times, and that we should toil in concert for a theory of the universe and of life, in order that thus we may arrive at a mental disposition which shall make us really and truly civilized men.

It was a great joy to me to be afforded the opportunity of putting forward, in the *Dale Lectures*, delivered in Oxford, the views on which this philosophy of civilization is based.

I would tender my deepest thanks to my friends, Mr. C. T. Campion, M.A., now of Grahamstown, South Africa, and Dr. J. P. Naish, of Oxford. Mr. Campion is the translator of this first part of the "Philosophy of Civilization". Dr. Naish has seen the book through the press and translated this preface.

ALBERT SCHWEITZER.

Strasbourg, Alsace.
February, 1923.

CONTENTS

CHAPTER I

xvi

THE DECAY AND THE RESTORATION OF CIVILIZATION

CHAPTER I

HOW PHILOSOPHY IS RESPONSIBLE FOR THE COLLAPSE OF CIVILIZATION

Our self-deception as to the real conditions of our civilization. The collapse of the theory of the universe on which our ideals were based. The superficial character of modern philosophizing.

WE are living to-day under the sign of the collapse of civilization. The situation has not been produced by the war; the latter is only a manifestation of it. The spiritual atmosphere has solidified into actual facts, which again react on it with disastrous results in every respect. This interaction of material and spiritual has assumed a most unhealthy character. Just below a mighty cataract we are driving along in a current full of formidable eddies, and it will need the most gigantic efforts to rescue the vessel of our fate from the dangerous side channel into which we have allowed it to drift, and bring it back into the main stream, if, indeed, we can hope to do so at all.

We have drifted out of the stream of civilization because there was amongst us no real reflection upon what civilization is. It is true that at the end of the last century and the beginning of this there appeared a number of works on civilization with the most varied titles ; but, as though in obedience to some secret order, they made no attempt to settle and make clear the conditions of our intellectual life, but devoted themselves exclusively to its origin and history. They gave us a relief map of civilization marked with roads which men had observed or invented, and which led us over hill and dale through the fields of history from the Renaissance to the twentieth century. It was a triumph for the historical sense of the authors. The crowds whom these works instructed were filled with satisfied contentment when they understood that their civilization was the organic product of so many centuries of the working of spiritual and social forces, but no one worked out and described the content of our spiritual life. No one tested its value from the point of view of the nobility of its ideas, and its ability to produce real progress.

Thus we crossed the threshold of the twentieth century with an unshakable conceit of ourselves, and whatever was written at that time about our civilization only confirmed us in our ingenuous belief in its high value. Anyone who expressed doubt was regarded with astonishment. Many, indeed, who were on the road to error, stopped and returned to the main road again because they were afraid of the path which led off to the side. Others continued along the main road, but in silence; the understanding and insight which were at work in them only condemned them to isolation.

It is clear now to everyone that the suicide of civilization is in progress. What yet remains of it is no longer safe. It is still standing, indeed, because it was not exposed to the destructive pressure which overwhelmed the rest, but, like the rest, is built upon rubble, and the next landslide will very likely carry it away.

But what was it that preceded and led up to this loss of power in the innate forces of civilization?

The age of the Illuminati and of rationalism had put forward ethical ideals, based on reason, concerning the development of the individual to true manhood, his position in society, the material and spiritual problems which arose out of society, the relations of the different nations to each other, and their issue in a humanity which should be united in

3

the pursuit of the highest moral and spiritual
objects. These ideals had begun, both in philosophy
and in general thought, to get into contact with
reality and to alter the general environment. In
the course of three or four generations there had
been such progress made, both in the ideas under-
lying civilization and in their material embodiment,
that the age of true civilization seemed to have
dawned upon the world and to be assured of an
uninterrupted development.

But about the middle of the nineteenth century
this mutual understanding and co-operation between
ethical ideals and reality began to break down, and
in the course of the next few decades it disappeared
more and more completely. Without resistance,
without complaint, civilization abdicated. Its ideas
lagged behind, as though they were too exhausted
to keep pace with it. How did this come about ?

*

*   *

The decisive element in the production of this
result was philosophy's renunciation of her duty.

In the eighteenth century and the early part of the
nineteenth it was philosophy which led and guided
thought in general. She had busied herself with
the questions which presented themselves to mankind at each successive period, and had kept the

4

thought of civilized man actively reflecting upon them. Philosophy at that time included within herself an elementary philosophizing about man, society, race, humanity and civilization, which produced in a perfectly natural way a living popular philosophy that controlled the general thought, and maintained the enthusiasm for civilization.

But that ethical, and at the same time optimistic, view of things in which the Illuminati and rationalism had laid the foundations of this healthy popular philosophy, was unable in the long run to meet the criticism levelled at it by pure thought. Its naïve dogmatism raised more and more prejudice against it. Kant tried to provide the tottering building with new foundations, undertaking to alter the rationalistic view of things in accordance with the demands of a deeper theory of knowledge, without, however, making any change in its essential spiritual elements. Goethe, Schiller and other intellectual giants of the age, showed, by means of criticism both kindly and malicious, that rationalism was rather popular philosophy than real philosophy, but they were not in a position to put into the place of what they destroyed anything new which could give the same effective support to the ideas about civilization which were current in the general thought of the time.

Fichte, Hegel, and other philosophers, who, for all their criticism of rationalism, paid homage to its ethical ideals, attempted to establish a similar ethical and optimistic view of things by speculative methods, that is by logical and metaphysical discussion of pure being and its development into a universe. For three or four decades they succeeded in deceiving themselves and others with this supposedly creative and inspiring illusion, and in doing violence to reality in the interests of their theory of the universe. But at last the natural sciences, which all this time had been growing stronger and stronger, rose up against them, and, with a plebeian enthusiasm for the truth of reality, reduced to ruins the magnificent creations of their imagination.

Since that time the ethical ideas on which civilization rests have been wandering about the world, poverty-stricken and homeless. No theory of the universe has been advanced which can give them a solid foundation; in fact, not one has made its appearance which can claim for itself solidity and inner consistency. The age of philosophic dogmatism had come definitely to an end, and after that nothing was recognized as truth except the science which described reality. General theories of the universe no longer appeared as fixed stars; they were regarded as resting on hypothesis, and ranked no higher than comets.

The same weapon which struck down the dogmatism of knowledge about the universe struck down also the dogmatic enunciation of spiritual ideas. The early simple rationalism, the critical rationalism of Kant, and the speculative rationalism of the great philosophers of the nineteenth century had all alike done violence to reality in two ways. They had given a position above that of the facts of science to the views which they had arrived at by pure thought, and they had also preached a series of ethical ideals which were meant to replace by new ones the various existing relations in the ideas and the material environment of mankind. When the first of these two forms of violence was proved to be a mistaken one, it became questionable whether the second could still be allowed the justification which it had hitherto enjoyed. The doctrinaire methods of thought which made the existing world nothing but material for the production of a purely theoretical sketch of a better future were replaced by sympathetic attempts to understand the historical origin of existing things for which Hegel's philosophy had prepared the way.

With a general mentality of this description, a real combination of ethical ideals with reality was no

longer possible ; there was not the freedom from
prejudice which that required, and so there came a
weakening of the convictions which were the driving
power of civilization. So, too, an end was put to
that justifiable violence to human convictions and
circumstances without which the reforming work of
civilization can make no advance, because it was
bound up with that other unjustifiable violence to
reality. That is the tragic element in the psycho-
logical development of our spiritual life during the
latter half of the nineteenth century.

Rationalism, then, had been dismissed ; but with
it went also the optimistic convictions as to the
moral meaning of the universe and of humanity, of
society and of man, to which it had given birth,
though the conviction still exerted so much influence
that no attention was paid to the catastrophe which
had really begun.

* * *

Philosophy did not realize that the power of the
ideas about civilization which had been entrusted
to it was becoming a doubtful quantity. At the end
of one of the most brilliant works on the history of
philosophy which appeared at the close of the nineteenth century philosophy is defined as the process
" by which there comes to completion, step by step,

8

and with ever clearer and surer consciousness, that conviction about the value of civilization the universal validity of which it is the object of philosophy itself to affirm." But the author has forgotten the essential point, viz., that there was a time when philosophy did not merely convince itself of the value of civilization, but also let its convictions go forth as fruitful ideas destined to influence the general thought, while from the middle of the nineteenth century onwards these convictions had become more and more of the nature of hoarded and unproductive capital.

Once philosophy had been an active worker producing universal convictions about civilization. Now, after the collapse in the middle of the nineteenth century, this same philosophy had become a mere drawer of dividends, concentrating her activities far from the world on what she had managed to save. She had become a mere science, which sifted the results of the historical and natural sciences, and collected from them material for a future theory of the universe, carrying on with this object in view a learned activity in all branches of knowledge. At the same time she became more and more absorbed in the study of her own past. Philosophy came to mean practically the history of philosophy, but the creative spirit had left her. She became more and

more a philosophy which contained no real thought.
She reflected, indeed, on the results achieved by the
individual sciences, but she lost the power of
thought about fundamental problems.

She looked back with condescending pity on the
rationalism which she had outstripped. She prided
herself on being able to trace her descent through
Kant, on having been shown by Hegel the inner
meaning of history, and on being at work to-day in
close sympathy with the natural sciences. But for
all that she was poorer than the poorest rationalism,
because she now carried on in imagination only, and
not in reality, the recognized work of philosophy,
which the latter had practised so zealously.
Rationalism, for all its simplicity, had been a
working philosophy, but philosophy herself had
now become, for all her insight, merely a pedantic
philosophy of degenerates. She still played, indeed,
some sort of *rôle* in schools and universities, but she
had no longer any message for the great world.

In spite of all her learning, she had become a
stranger to the world, and the problems of life which
occupied men and the whole thought of the age had
no part in her activities. Her way lay apart from
the general spiritual life, and just as she derived no
stimulus from the latter, so she gave none back.
Refusing to concern herself with fundamental

problems, she contained no fundamental philosophy which could become a philosophy of the
people.

From this impotence came the aversion to all
generally intelligible philosophizing which is so
characteristic of her. Popular philosophy was for
her merely a review, prepared for the use of the
crowd, simplified, and therefore rendered inferior,
of the results given by the individual sciences which
she had herself sifted and put together in view of a
future theory of the universe. She was wholly
unconscious of several things, viz., that there is a
popular philosophy which arises out of such a
review; that it is just the province of philosophy to
deal with the primary, deeper questions about which
individuals and the crowd are thinking, or ought to
be thinking, to apply to them more comprehensive
and more thorough methods of thought, and then
restore them to general currency; and, finally, that
the value of any philosophy is in the last resort to be
measured by its capacity, or incapacity, to trans-
form itself into a living philosophy of the people.

Whatever is deep is also simple, and can be
reproduced as such, if only its relation to the whole
of reality is preserved. It is then something
abstract, which secures for itself a many-sided life
as soon as it comes into contact with facts.

Whatever of inquiring thought there was among
the general public was therefore compelled to
languish, because our philosophy refused either to
acknowledge or to help it. It found in front of it a
deep chasm which it could not cross.

Of gold coinage, minted in the past, philosophy
had abundance ; hypotheses about a soon to be
developed theological theory of the universe filled
her vaults like unminted bullion ; but food with
which to appease the spiritual hunger of the present
she did not possess. Deceived by her own riches,
she had neglected to plant any ground with nourish-
ing crops, and therefore, ignoring the hunger of the
age, she left the latter to its fate.

That pure thought never managed to construct
a theory of the universe of an optimistic, ethical
character, and to build up on that for a foundation
the ideals which go to produce civilization, was not
the fault of philosophy ; it was a fact which became
evident as thought developed. But philosophy was
guilty of a wrong to our age in that it did not admit
the fact, but remained wrapped up in its illusion,
as though this were really a help to the progress of
civilization.

The ultimate vocation of philosophy is to be the
guide and guardian of the general reason, and it was
her duty, in the circumstances of the time, to confess

to our world that ethical ideals were no longer
supported by any general theory of the universe,
but were, till further notice, left to themselves, and
must make their way in the world by their own
innate power. She ought to have shown us that
we have to fight on behalf of the ideals on which our
civilization rests. She ought to have tried to give
these ideals an independent existence by virtue of
their own inner value and inner truth, and so to keep
them alive and active without any extraneous help
from a corresponding theory of the universe. No
effort should have been spared to direct the attention
of the cultured and the uncultured alike to the
problem of the ideals of civilization.

But philosophy philosophized about everything
except civilization. She went on working undeviat-
ingly at the establishment of a theoretical view of
the universe, as though by means of it everything
could be restored, and did not reflect that this theory,
even if it were completed, would be constructed only
out of history and science, and would accordingly
be unoptimistic and unethical, and would remain for
ever an " impotent theory of the universe," which
could never call forth the energies needed for the
establishment and maintenance of the ideals of
civilization.

So little did philosophy philosophize about

civilization that she did not even notice that she herself and the age along with her were losing more and more of it. In the hour of peril the watchman who ought to have kept us awake was himself asleep, and the result was that we put up no fight at all on behalf of our civilization.

CHAPTER II

HINDRANCES TO CIVILIZATION IN OUR ECONOMIC
AND SPIRITUAL LIFE

The unfree economic position of the modern man. The undeveloped condition of the modern man. The modern man's want of humanity. The lack of spiritual independence in the man of to-day.

EVEN if the abdication of thought has been, as we have seen, the decisive factor in the collapse of our civilization, there are yet a number of other causes which combine with it to hinder our progress in this regard. They are to be found in the field of spiritual as well as in that of economic activity, and depend, above all, on the interaction between the two, an interaction which is unsatisfactory and continually becoming more so.

The capacity of the modern man for progress in civilization is diminished because the circumstances in which he finds himself placed injure him psychically and stunt his personality.

The development of civilization comes about—to put it quite generally—by individual men thinking out ideals which aim at the progress of the whole, and then so fitting them to the realities of life that

they assume the shape in which they can influence
most effectively the circumstances of the time. A
man's ability to be a pioneer of progress, that is, to
understand what civilization is and to work for it,
depends, therefore, on his being a thinker and on his
being free. He must be the former if he is to be
capable of comprehending his ideals and putting
them into shape. He must be free in order to be in
a position to launch his ideals out into the general
life. The more completely his activities are taken
up in any way by the struggle for existence, the more
strongly will the impulse to improve his own condition find expression in the ideals of his thought.
Ideals of self-interest then get mixed up with and
spoil his ideals of civilization.

Material and spiritual freedom are closely bound
up with one another. Civilization presupposes free
men, for only by free men can it be thought out and
brought to realization.

But among mankind to-day both freedom and the
capacity for thought have been sadly diminished.

If society had so developed that a continually
widening circle of the population could enjoy a
modest, but well-assured, condition of comfort,
civilization would have been much more helped
than it has been by all the material conquests which
are lauded in its name. These do, indeed, make

mankind as a whole less dependent upon nature, but at the same time they diminish the number of free and independent lives. The artisan who was his own master becomes the factory hand through the compulsion of machinery. Because in the complicated business world of to-day only under-takings with abundant capital behind them can maintain their existence, the place of the small, independent dealer is being taken more and more completely by the employee. Even the classes which still possess a larger or smaller amount of property or maintain a more or less independent activity get drawn more and more completely into the struggle for existence because of the insecurity of present conditions under the economic system of to-day.

The lack of freedom which results is made worse still because the factory system creates continually growing agglomerations of people who are thereby compulsorily separated from the soil which feeds them, from their own homes and from nature. Hence comes serious psychical injury. There is only too much truth in the paradoxical saying that abnormal life begins with the loss of one's own field and dwelling-place.

Civilization is, it is true, furthered to a certain extent by the self-regarding ideals produced by the

groups of people who unite and co-operate in defence
of their similarly threatened interests in so far as
they seek to obtain an improvement in their material,
and thereby also in their spiritual, environment.
But these ideals are a danger to the idea of civilization as such, because the form which they assume
is either not at all, or very imperfectly, determined
by the really universal interests of the community.
The consideration of civilization as such is held
back by the competition between the various self-
regarding ideals which go under its name.

To the want of freedom we have to add the evil
of overwork.   For two or three generations numbers
of individuals have been living as workers merely,
not as human beings.   Whatever can be said in a
general way about the moral and spiritual significance of labour has no bearing on what they have
to do.   An excessive amount of labour is the rule
to-day in every department of industry, with the
result that the labourer's spiritual element cannot
possibly thrive.   This overwork hits him indirectly
even in his childhood, for his parents, caught in the
inexorable toils of work, cannot devote themselves
to his up-bringing as they should.   Thus his
development is robbed of something which can
never be made good, and later in life, when he himself is the slave of over-long hours, he feels more and

more the need of external distractions. To spend the time left to him for leisure in self-cultivation, or in serious intercourse with his fellows or with books, requires a mental collectedness and a self-control which he finds very difficult. Complete idleness, forgetfulness, and diversion from his usual activities are a physical necessity. He does not want to think, and seeks not self-improvement, but entertainment, that kind of entertainment, moreover, which makes least demand upon his spiritual faculties.

The mentality of this mass of individuals, spiritually relaxed and incapable of self-collectedness, reacts upon all those institutions which ought to serve the cause of culture, and therewith of civilization. The theatre takes a second place behind the pleasure resort or the picture show, and the instructive book behind the diverting one. An ever increasing proportion of periodicals and newspapers have to accommodate themselves to the necessity of putting their matter before their readers in the shape which lets it be assimilated most easily. A comparison of the average newspapers of to-day with those of fifty or sixty years ago shows how thoroughly such publications have had to change their methods in this respect.

When once the spirit of superficiality has pene-

c 2

trated into the institutions which ought to sustain
the spiritual life, these exercise on their part a
reflex influence on the society which they have
brought to this condition, and force on all alike this
state of mental vacuity.

How completely this want of thinking power has
become a second nature in men to-day is shown by
the kind of sociability which it produces. When
two of them meet for a conversation each is careful
to see that their talk does not go beyond generalities
or develop into a real exchange of ideas. No one
has anything of his own to give out, and everyone
is haunted by a sort of terror lest anything original
should be demanded from him.

The spirit produced in such a society of never-
concentrated minds is rising among us as an ever
growing force, and it results in a lowered conception
of what man should be. In ourselves, as in others,
we look for nothing but vigour in productive work,
and resign ourselves to the abandonment of any
higher ideal.

When we consider this want of freedom and of
mental concentration, we see that the conditions of
life for the inhabitants of our big cities are as
unfavourable as they could be. Naturally, then,
those inhabitants are in most danger on their
spiritual side. It is doubtful whether big cities

have ever been foci of civilization in the sense that
in them there has arisen the ideal of a man well and
truly developed as a spiritual personality ; to-day,
at any rate, the condition of things is such that true
civilization needs to be rescued from the spirit that
issues from them and their inhabitants.

*

*   *

But, besides the hindrance caused to civilization
by the modern man's lack of freedom and of the
power of mental concentration, there is a further
hindrance caused by his imperfect development.
The enormous increase of human knowledge and
power, in specialized thoroughness as well as in extent, necessarily leads to individual activities being
limited more and more to well-defined departments.
Human labour is organized and co-ordinated so
that specialization may enable individuals to make
the highest and most effective possible contribution.
The results obtained are amazing, but the spiritual
significance of the work for the worker suffers.
There is no call upon the whole man, only upon some
of his faculties, and this has a reflex effect upon his
nature as a whole. The faculties which build up
personality and are called out by comprehensive
and varied tasks are ousted by the less comprehensive ones, which from this point of view are, in the

21

general sense of the word, less spiritual. The artisan
of to-day does not understand his trade as a whole
in the way in which his predecessor did. He no
longer learns, like the latter, to work the wood or the
metal through all the stages of manufacture ; many
of these stages have already been carried out by
men and machines before the material comes into
his hands. Consequently his reflectiveness, his
imagination, and his skill are no longer called out
by ever varying difficulties in the work, and his
creative and artistic powers are atrophied. In
place of the normal self-consciousness which is
promoted by work into the doing of which he must
put his whole power of thought and his whole
personality, there comes a self-satisfaction which is
content with a fragmentary ability which, it may be
admitted, is perfect, and this self-satisfaction is
persuaded by its perfection in mastering details to
overlook its imperfection in dealing with the whole.

In all professions, most clearly perhaps in the
pursuit of science, we can recognize the spiritual
danger with which specialization threatens not only
individuals, but the spiritual life of the community.
It is already noticeable, too, that education is
carried on now by teachers who have not a wide
enough outlook to make their scholars understand
the interconnection of the individual sciences, and

to be able to give them a mental horizon as wide as it should be.

Then, as if specialization and the organization of work, where it is unavoidable, were not already injurious enough to the soul of the modern man, it is pursued and built up where it could be dispensed with. In administration, in education, and in every kind of calling the natural sphere of activity is narrowed as far as possible by rules and superintendence. How much less free in many countries is the elementary school teacher of to-day compared with what he was once! How lifeless and impersonal has his teaching become as a result of all these limitations!

Thus through our methods of work we have suffered loss spiritually and as individuals just in proportion as the material output of our collective activity has increased. Here, too, is an illustration of that tragic law which says that every gain brings with it, somehow or other, a corresponding loss.

*
* *

But man to-day is in danger not only through his lack of freedom, of the power of mental concentration, and of the opportunity for all-round development: he is in danger of losing his humanity.

The normal attitude of man to man is made very

difficult for us. Owing to the hurry in which we live, to the increased facilities for intercourse, and to the necessity for living and working with many others in an overcrowded locality, we meet each other continually, and in the most varied relations, as strangers. Our circumstances do not allow us to deal with each other as man to man, for the limitations placed upon the activities of the natural man are so general and so unbroken that we get accustomed to them, and no longer feel our mechanical, impersonal intercourse to be something that is unnatural. We no longer feel uncomfortable that in such a number of situations we can no longer be men among men, and at last we give up trying to be so, even when it would be possible and proper.

In this respect, too, the soul of the townsman is influenced most unfavourably by his circumstances, and that influence, in its turn, works most unfavourably on the mentality of society.

Thus we tend to forget our relationship with our fellows, and are on the path towards inhumanity. Wherever there is lost the consciousness that every man is an object of concern for us just because he is man, civilization and morals are shaken, and the advance to fully developed inhumanity is only a question of time.

As a matter of fact, the most utterly inhuman

thoughts have been current among us for two generations past in all the ugly clearness of language and with the authority of logical principles. There has been created a social mentality which discourages humanity in individuals. The courtesy produced by natural feeling disappears, and in its place comes a behaviour which shows entire indifference, even though it is decked out more or less thoroughly in a code of manners. The stand-offishness and want of sympathy which are shown so clearly in every way to strangers are no longer felt as being really rudeness, but pass for the behaviour of the man of the world. Our society has also ceased to allow to all men, as such, a human value and a human dignity; many sections of the human race have become merely raw material and property in human form. We have talked for decades with ever increasing light-mindedness about war and conquest, as if these were merely operations on a chess-board; how was this possible save as the result of a tone of mind which no longer pictured to itself the fate of individuals, but thought of them only as figures or objects belonging to the material world? When the war broke out the inhumanity within us had a free course. And what an amount of insulting stuff, some decently veiled, some openly coarse, about the coloured races, has made its appearance during the last decades, and passed for truth and

reason, in our colonial literature and our parliaments, and so become an element in general public
opinion ! Twenty years ago there was a discussion
in one of our Continental parliaments about some
deported negroes who had been allowed to die of
hunger and thirst ; and there was no protest or
comment when, in a statement from the tribune, it
was said that they " had been lost " (" *eingegangen* "
or " *crêvé* "), as though it were a question of cattle !

In the education and the school books of to-day
the duty of humanity is relegated to an obscure
corner, as though it were no longer true that it is the
first thing necessary in the training of personality,
and as if it were not a matter of great importance
to maintain it as a strong influence in our human
race against the influence of outer circumstances.
It has not been so always. There was a time when
it was a ruling influence not only in schools, but in
literature, even down to the book of adventures.
Defoe's hero, Robinson Crusoe, is continually
reflecting on the subject of humane conduct, and he
feels himself so responsible for loyalty to this duty
that when defending himself he is continually
thinking how he can sacrifice the smallest number
of human lives ; he is so faithful, indeed, to this duty
of humanity, that the story of his adventures
acquires thereby quite a peculiar character. Is

there among works of this kind to-day a single one
in which we shall find anything like it ?

*

*   *

Another hindrance to civilization to-day is the
over-organization of our public life.

While it is certain that a properly ordered
environment is the condition and, at the same time,
the result of civilization, it is also undeniable that,
after a certain point has been reached, external
organization is developed at the expense of spiritual
life. Personality and ideas are then subordinated
to institutions, when it is really these which ought to
influence the latter and keep them inwardly alive.

If a comprehensive organization is established in
any department of social life, the results are at first
magnificent, but after a time they fall off. It is the
already existing resources which are realized at the
start, but later on the destructive influence of such
organization on what is living and original is clearly
seen in its natural results, and the more consistently
the organization is enlarged, the more strongly its
effect is felt in the repression of creative and spiritual
activity. There are modern States which cannot
recover either economically or spiritually from the
paralysing effects of a concentration which dates
from a very early period of their history.

The conversion of a wood into a park and its
maintenance as such may be a step towards carrying
out several different objects, but it is all over then
with the rich vegetation which would assure its
future condition in nature's own way.

Political, religious and economic associations aim
to-day at forming themselves in such a way as will
combine the greatest possible inner cohesion with
the highest possible degree of external activity.
Constitution, discipline, and everything that belongs
to administration are brought to a perfection
hitherto unknown. They attain their object, but
just in proportion as they do so these centres of
activity cease to work as living organizations, and
come more and more to resemble perfected machines.
Their inner life loses in richness and variety because
the personalities of which they are composed must
needs decay in character.

Our whole spiritual life nowadays has its course
within organizations. From childhood up the man
of to-day has his mind so full of the thought of
discipline that he loses the sense of his own indivi-
duality and can only see himself as thinking in the
spirit of some group or other of his fellows. A
thorough discussion between one idea and another
or between one man and another, such as constituted
the greatness of the eighteenth century, is never met

with now. But at that time fear of public opinion
was a thing unknown. All ideas had then to justify
themselves to the individual reason. To-day it is
the rule—and no one questions it—always to take
into account the views which prevail in organized
society. The individual starts by taking it for
granted that both for himself and his neighbours
there are certain views already established which they
cannot hope to alter, views which are determined
by nationality, creed, political party, social position,
and other elements in one's surroundings. These
views are protected by a kind of taboo, and are not
only kept sacred from criticism, but are not a
legitimate subject of conversation. This kind of
intercourse, in which we mutually abjure our
natural quality as thinking beings, is euphemistically
described as respect for other people's convictions,
as if there could be any convictions at all where
there is no thought.

The modern man is lost in the mass in a way
which is without precedent in history, and this is
perhaps the most characteristic trait in him. His
diminished concern about his own nature makes
him as it is susceptible, to an extent that is almost
pathological, to the views which society and its
organs of expression have put, ready made, into
circulation. Since, over and above this, society,

with its well-constructed organization, has become
a power of as yet unknown strength in the spiritual
life, man's want of independence in the face of it
has become so serious that he is almost ceasing to
claim a spiritual existence of his own. He is like
a rubber ball which has lost its elasticity, and pre-
serves indefinitely every impression that is made
upon it. He is under the thumb of the mass, and he
draws from it the opinions on which he lives,
whether the question at issue is national or political
or one of his own belief or unbelief.

Yet this abnormal subjection to external influences does not strike him as being a weakness. He
looks upon it as an achievement, and in his unlimited
spiritual devotion to the interests of the community
he thinks he is preserving the greatness of the modern
man. He intentionally exaggerates our natural
social instincts into something fantastically great.

It is just because we thus renounce the indefea-
sible rights of the individual that our race can
neither produce new ideas nor make current ones
serviceable for new objects ; its only experience is
that prevailing ideas obtain more and more authority, take on a more and more one-sided development, and live on till they have produced their last
and most dangerous consequences.

Thus we have entered on a new mediæval period.

The general determination of society has put freedom of thought out of fashion, because the majority renounce the privilege of thinking as free personalities, and let themselves be guided in everything by those who belong to the various groups and cliques.

Spiritual freedom, then, we shall recover only when the majority of individuals become once more spiritually independent and self-reliant, and discover their natural and proper relation to those organizations in which their souls have been entangled. But liberation from the Middle Ages of to-day will be a much more difficult process than that which freed the peoples of Europe from the first Middle Ages. The struggle then was against external authority established in the course of history. To-day the task is to get the mass of individuals to work themselves out of the condition of spiritual weakness and dependence to which they have brought themselves. Could there be a harder task ?

Moreover, no one as yet clearly perceives what a condition of spiritual poverty is ours to-day. Every year the spread of opinions which have no thought behind them is carried further by the masses, and the methods of this process have been so perfected, and have met with such a ready welcome, that our

confidence in being able to raise to the dignity of
public opinion the silliest of statements, wherever
it seems necessary to get them currently accepted,
has no need to justify itself before acting.

During the war the control of thought was made
complete. Propaganda definitely took the place of
truth.

With independence of thought thrown overboard,
we have, as was inevitable, lost our faith in truth.
Our spiritual life is disorganized, for the over-
organization of our external environment leads to
the organization of our absence of thought.

Not only in the intellectual sphere, but in the
moral also, the relation between the individual
and the community has been upset. With the
surrender of his own personal opinion the modern
man surrenders also his personal moral judgment.
In order that he may find good what the mass
declares to be such, whether in word or deed, and
may condemn what it declares to be bad, he sup-
presses the scruples which stir in him. He does not
allow them to find utterance either with others or
with himself. There are no stumbling-blocks which
his feeling of unity with the herd does not enable
him to surmount, and thus he loses his judgment in
that of the mass, and his own morality in theirs.

Above all, he is thus made capable of excusing

everything that is meaningless, cruel, unjust, or bad in the behaviour of his nation. Unconsciously to themselves, the majority of the members of our barbarian civilised States give less and less time to reflection as moral personalities, so that they may not be continually coming into inner conflict with their fellows as a body, and continually having to get over things which they feel to be wrong.

Public opinion helps them by popularizing the idea that the actions of the community are not to be judged so much by the standards of morality as by those of expediency, but they suffer injury to their souls. If we find among men of to-day only too few whose human and moral sensibility is still undamaged, the chief reason is that the majority have offered up their personal morality on the altar of their country, instead of remaining at variance with the mass and acting as a force which impels the latter along the road to perfection.

Not only between the economic and the spiritual, then, but also between the mass of men and individuals, there has developed a condition of unfavourable action and reaction. In the days of rationalism and serious philosophy the individual got help and support from society through the general confidence in the victory of the rational and moral, which society never failed to acknowledge

as something which explained and justified itself.
Individuals were then carried along by the mass ;
we are stifled by it. The bankruptcy of the civilized State, which becomes more manifest every
decade, is ruining the man of to-day. The demoralization of the individual by the mass is in full swing.

The man of to-day pursues his dark journey in a
time of darkness, as one who has no freedom, no
mental collectedness, no all-round development, as
one who loses himself in an atmosphere of inhumanity, who surrenders his spiritual independence
and his moral judgment to the organized society in
which he lives, and who finds himself in every direction
up against hindrances to the temper of true civilization. Of the dangerous position in which he is placed
philosophy has no understanding, and therefore
makes no attempt to help him. She does not even
urge him to reflection on what is happening to himself.

The terrible truth that with the progress of
history and the economic development of the world
it is becoming not easier, but harder, to develop true
civilization, has never found utterance.

CHAPTER III

CIVILIZATION ESSENTIALLY ETHICAL IN CHARACTER

What is civilization ? Origin of the unethical conception of civilization. Our sense of reality. Our historical sense. Nationalism. National civilization. Our misleading trust in facts and organization. The true sense for reality.

THIS question ought to have been pressing itself on the attention of all men who consider themselves civilized, but it is remarkable that in the world's literature generally one hardly finds that it has been put at all until to-day, and still more rarely is any answer given. It was supposed that there was no need for a definition of civilization, since we already possessed the thing itself. If the question was ever touched upon, it was considered to be sufficiently settled with references to history and the present day. But now, when events are bringing us inexorably to the consciousness that we live in a dangerous medley of civilization and barbarism, we must, whether we wish to or not, try to determine the nature of true civilization.

For a quite general definition we may say that civilization is progress, material and spiritual progress, on the part of individuals as of the mass.

D 2

In what does it consist ? First of all in a lessening of the strain imposed on individuals and on the mass by the struggle for existence. The establishment of as favourable conditions of living as possible for all is a demand which must be made partly for its own sake, partly with a view to the spiritual and moral perfecting of individuals, which is the ultimate object of civilization.

The struggle for existence is a double one : man has to assert himself in nature and against nature, and similarly also among his fellow-men and against them.

A diminution of the struggle is secured by strengthening the supremacy of reason over both external nature and human nature, and making it subserve as accurately as possible the ends proposed.

Civilization is then twofold in its nature : it realizes itself in the supremacy of reason, first, over the forces of nature, and, secondly, over the dispositions of men.

Which of these kinds of progress is most truly progress in civilization ? The latter, though it is the least open to observation. Why ? For two reasons. First, the supremacy which we secure by reason over external nature represents not unqualified progress, but a progress which brings with its advantages also disadvantages which may work in the direction of barbarism. The reason why the economic circumstances of our time endanger our civilization is to be sought for partly in the fact that we have pressed into our service natural forces which can be embodied in machines. But with that there must be such a supremacy of reason over the dispositions of men that they, and the nations which they form, will not use against one another the power which the control of these forces gives them, and thus plunge one another into a struggle for existence which is far more terrible than that between men in a state of nature.

A normal claim to be civilized can, then, only be reckoned as valid when it recognizes this distinction between what is essential in civilization and what is not.

Both kinds of progress can, indeed, be called spiritual in the sense that they both rest upon a spiritual activity in man, yet we may call the supremacy over natural forces material progress because in it material objects are mastered and turned to man's use. The supremacy of reason over human dispositions, on the other hand, is a spiritual achievement in another sense, in that it means the working of spirit upon spirit, *i.e.*, of one section of the power of reflexion upon another section of it.

And what is meant by the supremacy of the reason over human dispositions ? It means that both individuals and the mass let their willing be determined by the material and spiritual good of the whole and the individuals that compose it ; that is to say, their actions are ethical. Ethical progress is, then, that which is truly of the essence of civilization, and has only one significance ; material progress is that which is not of the essential at all, and may have a twofold effect on the development of civilization. This moral conception of civilization will strike some people as rationalistic and old-fashioned. It accords better with the spirit of our times to conceive of civilization as a natural manifestation of life in the course of human evolution, but one with most interesting complications. We are concerned, however, not with what is ingenious, but with what is true. In this case the simple is the true—the inconvenient truth with which it is our laborious task to deal.

*

* *

The attempts to distinguish between civilization as what the Germans call " Kultur " and civilization as mere material progress aim at making the world familiar with the idea of an unethical form of civilization side by side with the ethical, and at clothing the former with a word of historical meaning. But nothing in the history of the word " civilization " justifies such attempts. The word, as commonly used hitherto, means the same as the German " Kultur ", viz., the development of man to a state of higher organization and a higher moral standard. Some languages prefer one word; others prefer the other. The German usually speaks of "Kultur", the Frenchman usually of "civilisation", but the establishment of a difference between them is justified neither philologically nor historically. We can speak of ethical and unethical "Kultur" or of ethical and unethical "civilisation", but not of "Kultur" and "civilisation".

But how did it come about that we lost the idea that the ethical has a decisive meaning and value as part of civilization?

All attempts at civilization hitherto have been a matter of processes in which the forces of progress were at work in almost every department of life. Great achievements in art, architecture, administration, economics, industry, commerce, and colonization succeeded each other with a spiritual impetus which produced a higher conception of the universe. Any ebb of the tide of civilization made itself felt in the material sphere as well as in the ethical and spiritual, earlier, as a rule, in the former than in the latter. Thus in Greek civilization there set in as early as the time of Aristotle an incomprehensible arrest of science and political achievement, whereas the ethical movement only reached its completion in the following centuries in that great work of education which was undertaken in the ancient world by the Stoic philosophy. In the Chinese, Indian and Jewish civilizations ability in dealing with material things was from the start, and always remained, at a lower level than the spiritual and ethical efforts of these races.

In the movement of civilization which began with the Renaissance, there were both material and spiritual-ethical forces of progress at work side by side, as though in rivalry with each other, and this continued down to the beginning of the nineteenth century. Then, however, something unprecedented happened : man's ethical energy died away, while the conquests achieved by his spirit in the material sphere increased by leaps and bounds. Thus for several decades our civilization enjoyed the great advantages of its material progress while as yet it hardly felt the consequences of the dying down of the ethical movement. People lived on in the conditions produced by that movement without seeing clearly that their position was no longer a tenable one and preparing to face the storm that was brewing in the relations between the nations and within the nations themselves. In this way our own age, having never taken the trouble to reflect, arrived at the opinion that civilization consists primarily in scientific, technical and artistic achievements, and that it can reach its goal without ethics, or, at any rate, with a minimum of them.

Public opinion bowed down before this merely external conception of civilization because it was exclusively represented by persons whose position in society and scientific culture seemed to show them to be competent to judge in matters of the spiritual life.

*

*   *

What was the result of our giving up the ethical conception of civilization, and therewith all attempts to bring reasoned ethical ideals into effective relation with reality ? It was that instead of using thought to produce ideals which fitted in with reality, we left reality without any ideals at all. Instead of discussing together the essential elements, such as population, State, Church, society, progress, which decide the character of our social development and that of mankind generally, we contented ourselves with starting from what is given by experience. Only forces and tendencies which were already at work were to be considered. Fundamental truths and convictions which ought to produce logical or ethical compulsion we would no longer acknowledge. We refused to believe that any ideas could be applicable to reality except those derived from experience. Thus ideals which had been knowingly and intentionally lowered domi-nated our spiritual life and the whole world.

How we glorified our practical common-sense, which was to give us such power in dealing with the world ! Yet we were behaving, really, like boys who give themselves up exultingly to the forces of nature and whizz down a hill on their toboggan without asking themselves whether they will be able to steer their vehicle successfully when they come to the next bend or the next unexpected obstacle.

It is only a conviction which is based upon reasoned ethical ideals that is capable of producing free activity, *i.e.*, activity deliberately planned with a view to its object. In proportion as ideals taken from the workaday world are combined with it, reality influences reality. But then the human soul acts merely as an agent of debasing change.

Events which are to produce practical results within us are worked upon and moulded by our mentality. This mentality has a certain character, and on that character depends the nature of those value-judgments which rule our relation to facts.

Normally this character is to be found in the reasoned ideas which our reflection upon reality brings into existence. If these disappear there is not left a void in which " events in themselves " can affect us, but the control of our mentality passes now to the opinions and feelings which hitherto have been ruled and kept under by our reasoned ideas. When the virgin forest is cut down, brushwood springs up where the big trees were formerly. Whenever our great convictions are destroyed their place is taken by smaller ones which carry out in inferior fashion the functions of the former.

With the giving up of ethical ideals which accompanies our passion for reality our practical efficiency is not, therefore, improved, but diminished. It does not make the man of to-day a cool observer and calculator such as he supposes himself to be, for he is under the influence of opinions and emotions which are created in him by facts. All unconsciously he mixes with what is the work of his reason so much of what is emotional that the one spoils the other. Within this circle move the judgments and impulses of our society, whether we deal with the largest questions or the smallest. Individuals and nations alike, we deal indiscriminately with real and imaginary values, and it is just this confused medley of real and unreal, of sober thought and capacity for enthusiasm for the unmeaning, that makes the mentality of the modern man so puzzling and so dangerous.

Our sense of reality, then, means this, that, as a result of emotional and short-sighted calculations of advantage, we let one fact issue immediately in another, and so on indefinitely. As we are not consciously aiming at any definitely planned goal, our activity may really be described as a kind of natural happening.

43

We react to facts in the most irrational way. Without plan or foundations we build our future into the circumstances of the time and leave it exposed to the destructive effects of the chaotic jostling that goes on amongst them. " Firm ground at last "! we cry, and sink helpless in the stream of events.

*

*   *

The blindness with which we endure this fate is made worse by our belief in our historical sense, which, in this connection, is nothing else than our sense of reality prolonged backwards. We believe ourselves to be a critical generation which, thanks to its thorough knowledge of the past, is in a position to understand the direction which events are destined to take from the present to the future. We add to the ideals which have been taken from existing reality others which we borrow from history.

The achievements of historical science reached by the nineteenth century do, indeed, deserve our admiration, but it is another question whether our generation, for all its possession of an historical science, possesses a true historical sense.

Historical sense, in the full meaning of the term, implies a critical objectivity in the face of far-off and recent events alike. To keep this faculty free from the bias of opinions and interests when we are estimating facts is a power which even our historians do not possess. As long as they are dealing with a period so remote that it has no bearing on the present they are critical so far as the views of the school to which they belong allow it. But if the past stands in any real connection with " to-day ", we can perceive at once in their estimate the influence of their particular standpoint, rational, religious, social or economic.

It is significant that while during the last few decades the learning of our historians has, no doubt, increased, their critical objectivity has not. Previous investigators kept this ideal before their eyes in much greater purity than have those of to-day ; we have gone so far that we no longer seriously make the demand that in scientific dealings with the past there shall be a suppression of all prejudices which spring from nationality or creed. It is quite common nowadays to see the greatest learning bound up with the strongest bias. In our historical literature the highest positions are occupied by works written with propagandist aims.

So little educative influence has science had on our historians that they have often espoused as passionately as anyone the opinions of their own people instead of calling the latter to a thoughtful estimate of the facts, as was their duty to their profession ; they have remained nothing but men

45

of learning. They have not even started on the task for which they entered the service of civilization, and the hopes of civilization, which in the middle of the nineteenth century rested on the rise of a science of history, have been as little fulfilled as those which were bound up with the demand for national States and democratic forms of government.

The generation that has been brought up by teachers such as these has naturally not much idea of an elevated or active conception of events. Accurately viewed, its characteristic feature is not so much that we understand our past better than earlier generations understood theirs, but rather that we attribute to the past an extraordinarily increased meaning for the present. Now and again we actually substitute it for the latter. It is not enough for us that what has been is present in its results in what now is ; we want to have it always with us, and to feel ourselves determined by it.

In this effort to be continually experiencing our historical process of becoming, and to acknowledge it, we replace our normal relation to the past by an artificial one, and wishing to find within the past the whole of our present, we misuse it in order to deduce from it, and to legitimize by an appeal to it, our claims, our opinions, our feelings and our passions. Under the very eyes of our historical learning there springs up a manufactured history for popular use, in which the current national and confessional ideas are unreservedly approved and upheld, and our school history books become regular culture beds of historical lies.

The misuse of history is a necessity for us. The ideas and dispositions which rule us cannot be justified by reason ; nothing is left for us but to give them foundations in history.

It is significant that we have no real interest in what is valuable in the past. Its great spiritual achievements are mechanically registered, but we do not let ourselves be touched by them. Still less do we accept them as a heritage ; nothing has any value for us except what can be squared with our plans, passions, feelings, and æsthetic moods of to-day. With these we live ourselves by lies into the past, and then assert with unshaken assurance that we have our roots in it.

This is the character of the reverence we pay to history. Blinded by what we consider or declare to be past and done with, we lose all sense for what is to happen, so that of nothing can we say: " It is finished," nothing now gets accomplished. Again and again we let what is past rise up artificially in what is present, and endow bygone facts with a persistence of being which makes wholly impossible the normal development of our peoples. Just as our sense of reality makes us lose ourselves in present-day events, so does our historical sense compel us to do the same in those of the past.

*

 *   *

From these two things, our sense of reality and our historical sense, is born the nationalism to which we must refer the external catastrophe in which the decadence of our civilization finds its completion.

What is nationalism ? It is an ignoble patriotism, exaggerated till it has lost all meaning, which bears the same relation to the noble and healthy kind as the fixed idea of an imbecile does to normal conviction.

How does it develop among us ?

About the beginning of the nineteenth century the course of thought gave the national State its rightful position, starting for this from the axiom that it, as a natural and homogeneous organism, was better calculated than any other to make the ideal of the civilized State a working reality. In Fichte's addresses to the German nation the nation-State is summoned to the bar of the moral reason and learns that it has to submit in all things to the latter. It gives the necessary promise and straightway receives a commission to bring the civilized State into existence. It is given emphatically to understand that it must recognize as its highest task the continuous and steady development of the purely human element in the nation's life. It is to seek greatness by representing the ideas which can bring healing to the nations. Its citizens are urged to show their membership of it not through the lower, but through the higher, patriotism, that is, not to overvalue its external greatness and power, but to be careful to take for their aim " the unfolding of what is eternal and Godlike in the world," and to see that their objects coincide with the highest aims of humanity. Thus national feeling is placed under the guardianship of reason, morality and civilization. The cult of patriotism as such is to be considered as barbarism ; it does, indeed, announce itself to be such by the purposeless wars which it necessarily brings in its train.

In this way the idea of nationality was raised to the level of a valuable ideal of civilization. When civilization began to decline, its other ideals all fell also, but the idea of nationality maintained itself because it had transferred itself to the sphere of reality. It incorporated henceforward all that remained of civilization, and became the ideal which summed up all others. Here, then, we have the explanation of the mentality of our age, which concentrates all the enthusiasm of which it is capable on the idea of nationality, and believes itself to possess in that all moral and spiritual good things.

But with the decay of civilization the character of the idea of nationality changed. The guardianship exercised over it by the other moral ideals to which it had hitherto been subordinate now ceased, since these were themselves on trial, and the nationalist idea began a career of independence. It asserted, of course, that it was working in the service of civilization, but it was, in truth, only an idea of reality with a halo of civilization round it, and it was guided by no ethical ideals, but only by the instincts which deal with reality.

That reason and morality shall not be allowed to contribute a word to the formation of nationalist ideas and aspirations is demanded by the mass of men to-day as a sparing of their holiest feelings.

If in earlier times the decay of civilization did not produce any such confusion in the sentiments of the various nations, this was because the idea of nationality had not then been raised in the same way to be the ideal of civilization. It was, therefore, impossible that it should insinuate itself into the place of the true ideals of civilization, and through abnormal nationalist conceptions and dispositions bring into active existence an elaborate system of uncivilization.

That in nationalism we have to do not so much with things as with the unhealthy way in which they are dealt with in the imagination of the crowd, is clear from its whole behaviour. It claims to be following a policy of practical results (Realpolitik) ; in reality it by no means represents the uncompromisingly businesslike view of all the questions of home and foreign policy, but side by side with its egoism displays a certain amount of enthusiasm. Its practical policy is an over-valuation of certain questions of territorial economic interests, an over-valuation which has been elevated to a dogma and idealized, and is now supported by popular sentiment. It fights for its demands without having established any properly thought-out calculation of their real value. In order to be able to dispute the possession of millions of value, the modern State loaded itself with armaments costing hundreds of millions. Meaning to care for the protection and extension of its trade, it loaded the latter with imposts which imperilled its power of competing with its rivals much more than did any of the measures taken by those rivals.

Its practical politics were, therefore, in truth impracticable politics, because they allowed popular sentiment to come in, and thereby made the simplest questions insoluble. This style of politics put economic interests in the shop window, while it kept in the warehouse the ideas about greatness and conquest which belong to nationalism.

E 2

Every civilized State, in order to increase its power, gathered allies wherever it could. Thus half-civilized and uncivilized races were summoned by civilized ones to fight against the civilized neighbours of the latter, and these helpers were not content with the subordinate *rôle* which had been assigned to them. They acquired more and more influence on the course of events, till they were at last in a position to decide when the civilized nations of Europe should begin to fight each other about them. Thus has Nemesis come upon us for abandoning our wishes and betraying to the uncivilized world all that we still possessed of things that were of universal value.

It was significant of the unhealthy character of nationalism's " practical " politics that it tried in every possible way to deck itself out with a tinsel imitation of idealism. The struggle for power became one for right and civilization ; the alliances for the promotion of their selfish interests which various nations made with one another against all the rest were made to appear to be friendships and spiritual affinities. As such they were dated back into the past, even though history had a great deal more to say about hereditary quarrels than about spiritual relationships.

*

*　　　*

Finally, nationalism was not content with putting aside, in the sphere of politics generally, all attempts to bring into existence a really civilized humanity; it distorted the very idea of civilization itself and talked of national civilization.

Once there was what was known just simply as civilization, and every civilized nation strove to possess it in its purest and most fully developed form. In this respect nationality had in the idea of civilization at that time something much more original and less spoilt than it has in the same idea to-day. If, in spite of this, there was no impulse among the nations to separate the spiritual life of each from that of its neighbours, we have a proof that nationality is not in itself the strong element in the people that demanded this. Such a claim as is made to-day to have a *national civilization* is an unhealthy phenomenon. It presupposes that the civilized peoples of to-day have lost their healthy nature, and no longer follow instincts, but theories. They percuss and sound their souls to such an extent that these are no longer capable of any natural action. They analyse and describe them so continuously that in thinking of what they ought to be they forget what they actually are. Questions of spiritual differences between races are discussed so subtly, and with such obstinacy and dogmatism, that the talk works like an obsession, and the

53

peculiarities that are said to exist make their appearance like imaginary diseases.

In every department of life more and more effort is devoted to making clearly visible in the results which follow from them the emotions, the ideas, and the reasonings of the mass of the people. Any peculiarity preserved and fostered in this way shows that its natural counterpart has perished. The individual element in the personality of a people no longer, as something unconscious or half conscious, plays with varying lights on the totality of the nation's spiritual life. It becomes an artifice, a fashion, a self-advertisement, a mania. There is bred in the nation a mass of thought, the serious results of which in every department become more evident year by year. The spiritual life of some of the leading civilized nations has already, in comparison with earlier days, taken on a monotonous tone such as makes an observer feel anxious.

The unnatural character of this development shows itself not only in its results, but in the part which it allows to be played by conceit, self-importance, and self-deception. Anything valuable in a personality or a successful undertaking is attributed to some special excellence in the national character. Foreign soil is assumed to be incapable of producing the same or anything similar, and in most countries this vanity has grown to such a height that the greatest follies are no longer beyond its reach.

It goes without saying that there follows a serious decline in the spiritual element in the national civilization. The spirituality is, moreover, only a kind of disguise; it has in reality an avowedly materialist character. It is a distillation from all the external achievements of the nation in question and appears in partnership with its economic and political demands. While alleged to be grounded in the national peculiarities, nationalist civilization will not, as we should normally expect, remain limited to the nation itself; it feels called upon to impose itself upon others and make them happy! Modern nations seek markets for their civilization, as they do for their manufactures!

National civilization, therefore, is matter for propaganda and for export, and the necessary publicity is secured by liberal expenditure. The necessary phrases can be obtained ready-made and need only be strung together. Thus the world has inflicted on it a competition between national civilizations, and between these civilization itself comes off badly.

The nations of Europe entered the Middle Ages side by side as the heirs of the Greco-Roman world, and lived side by side with the freest mutual intercourse through the Renaissance, the period of the

Illuminati, and of the philosophy of more recent times. But we no longer believe that they, with their offshoots in the other continents, form an indivisible unit of civilization. If, however, in this latest age, the differences in their spiritual life have begun to stand out more distinctly, the cause of it is that the level of civilization has sunk. When the tide ebbs, shallows which separate bodies of deep water become visible ; while the tide is flowing they are out of sight.

How closely the nations which form the great body of civilized humanity are still interrelated spiritually is shown by the fact that they have all side by side suffered the same decadence.

*

*   *

With our sense of reality is bound up, further, the false confidence which we have in facts. We live in an atmosphere of optimism, as if the contradictions which show themselves in the world arranged themselves automatically so as to promote well-thought-out progress, and reconciled themselves in syntheses in which the valuable parts of the thesis and the antithesis coalesced.

In justification of this optimism appeal is made, both rightly and wrongly, to Hegel. It cannot be denied that he is the spiritual father of our sense of reality ; he is the first thinker who tried to be just to things as they exist. We have been trained by him to realize the method of progress in thesis, antithesis, and synthesis as they show themselves in the course of events. But his optimism was not a simple optimism about facts, as ours is. He lived still in the spiritual world of rationalism, and believed in the power of ethical ideas worked out by reason ; that was why he believed also in the certainty of uninterrupted spiritual progress. And it was because this was something upon which he could rely that he undertook to show how it was to be seen in the successive phases of events, and at the same time how it made itself a reality in the stream of outward facts. By emphasizing, however, the progressive purpose, which he finds immanent in the course of events, so strongly that it is possible to forget the ethical-spiritual presuppositions of his belief in progress, he is preparing the way for the despiritualized optimism about reality which has for decades been misleading us. Between the facts themselves there is nothing but an endless series of contradictions. The fresh mediating fact in which they counteract each other so as to make progress possible they cannot of themselves produce. This fact can only assert itself if the contradictions resolve themselves in a reasoned view in which there are ethical ideas about the condition of things which

57

it is sought to realize. These are the formative principles for the new element which is to arise out of the contradictories, and it is only in this reasoned ethical view that the latter cease to be blind, leading to no issue.

It was because we assumed the existence of principles, of progress, in the facts, that we viewed the advance of history, in which our future was being prepared, as progress in civilization, even though evolution condemned our optimism. And even now, when facts of the most terrible character cry out loudly against it, we shrink from giving up our creed. It no longer, indeed, gives us any real enlightenment, but the alternative, which bases optimism on belief in the ethical spirit, means such a revolution in our mode of thought that we find it difficult to take it into consideration.

With our reliance upon facts is bound up our reliance on organizations. The activities and the aims of our time are penetrated by a kind of obsession that if we could only succeed in perfecting or reforming in one direction or another the institutions of our public and social life, the progress demanded by civilization would begin of itself. We are, indeed, far enough from unanimity as to the plan needed for the reform of our arrangements : one section sketches out an anti-democratic plan ;

others believe that our mistake lies in the fact that democratic principles have not yet been applied consistently ; others, again, see salvation only in a Socialist or Communist organization of society. But all agree in attributing our present condition, with its absence of true civilization, to a failure of our institutions ; all look for the attainment of such civilization to a new organization of society ; all unite in thinking that with new institutions there would arise a new spirit.

*

*　　　　*

In this terrible confusion are entangled not only the unreflecting masses, but also many of the most earnest amongst us. The materialism of our age has reversed the relation between the spiritual and the actual. It believes that something with spiritual value can result from the working of facts. It was even expected that the war would bring us a spiritual regeneration ! In reality, however, the relation between them works in the opposite direction. A spiritual element of real value can, if it is present, influence the moulding of reality so as to bring about desired results, and can thus produce facts in support of itself. All institutions and organizations have only a relative significance. With the most diverse social and political

59

arrangements, the various civilized nations have all sunk to the same depth of barbarism. What we have experienced, and are still experiencing, must surely convince us that the spirit is everything and that institutions count for very little. Our institutions are a failure because the spirit of barbarism is at work in them. The best planned improvements in the organization of our society (though we are quite right in trying to secure them) cannot help us at all until we become at the same time capable of imparting a new spirit to our age.

The difficult problems with which we have to deal, even those which lie entirely in the material and economic sphere, are in the last resort only to be solved by an inner change of character. The wisest reforms in organization can only carry them a little nearer solution, never to the goal. The only conceivable way of bringing about a reconstruction of our world on new lines is first of all to become new men ourselves under the old circumstances, and then as a society in a new frame of mind so to smooth out the opposition between nations that a condition of true civilization may again become possible. Everything else is more or less wasted labour, because we are thereby building not on the spirit, but on what is merely external.

In the sphere of human events which decide the future of mankind reality consists in an inner conviction, not in given outward facts. Firm ground for our feet we find in reasoned ethical ideals. Are we going to draw from the spirit strength to create new conditions and turn our faces again to civilization, or are we going to continue to draw our spirit from our surroundings and go down with it to ruin ? That is the fateful question with which we are confronted.

The true sense for reality is that insight which tells us that only through ethical ideas about things can we arrive at a normal relation to reality. Only so can man and society win all the power over events that they are able to use. Without that power we are, whatever we may choose to do, delivered over into bondage to them.

What is going on to-day between nations and within them throws a glaring illumination upon this truth. The history of our time is characterized by a lack of reason which has no parallel in the past. Future historians will one day analyse this history in detail, and test by means of it their learning and their freedom from prejudice. But for all future times there will be, as there is for to-day, only one explanation, viz., that we sought to live and to carry on with a civilization which had no ethical principle behind it.

CHAPTER IV

THE WAY TO THE RESTORATION OF CIVILIZATION

Civilization-ideals have become powerless. Evolution and decay in the history of civilization. The reform of institutions and the reform of convictions. The individual as the sole agent of the restoration of civilization. The difficulties which beset the restoration of civilization.

THE ethical conception of civilization, then, is the only one that can be justified.

But where is the road that can bring us back from barbarism to civilization ? Is there such a road at all ?

The unethical conception of civilization answers : " No." To it all symptoms of decay are symptoms of old age, and civilization, just like any other natural process of growth, must after a certain period of time reach its final end. There is nothing, therefore, for us to do, so it says, but to take the causes of this as quite natural, and do our best at any rate to find interesting the unedifying phenomena of its senility, which testify to the gradual loss of the ethical character of civilization.

In the thinking then which surrenders itself to our sense of reality, optimism and pessimism are inextricably intermingled. If our optimism about reality is proved untenable, the optimism which thinks that continuous progress evolves itself among the facts as such, then the spirit which from above contemplates and analyses the situation turns without much concern to the mild pessimistic supposition that civilization has reached its Indian summer.

The ethical spirit cannot join in this little game of " Optimism or pessimism ? " It sees the symptoms of decay as what they really are, viz., something terrible. It asks itself with a shudder what will become of the world if this dying process really goes on unchecked. The condition of civilization is a source of pain to it, for civilization is not an object which it is interesting to analyse, but the hope on which its thoughts fly out over the future existence of the race. Belief in the possibility of a renewal of civilization is an actual part of its life ; that is why it can no longer quiet itself with what contents the sense of reality as it hovers between optimism and pessimism.

Those who regard the decay of civilization as something quite normal and natural console themselves with the thought that it is not civilization, but *a* civilization, which is falling a prey to dissolution ; that there will be a new age and a new race in which there will blossom a new civilization. But that is a mistake. The earth no longer has in reserve, as it had once, gifted peoples as yet unused, who can relieve us and take our place in some distant future as leaders of the spiritual life. We already know all those which the earth has to dispose of. There is not one among them which is not already taking such a part in our civilization that its spiritual fate is determined by our own. All of them, the gifted and the ungifted, the distant and the near, have felt the influence of those forces of barbarism which are at work among us. All of them are, like ourselves, diseased, and only as we recover can they recover.

It is not the civilization of a race, but that of mankind, present and future alike, that we must give up as lost, if belief in a rebirth of our civilization is a vain thing.

But it need not be so given up. If the ethical is the essential element in civilization, decadence changes into renaissance as soon as ethical activities are set to work again in our convictions and in the ideas which we undertake to stamp upon reality. The attempt to bring this about is well worth making, and it should be world-wide.

It is true that the difficulties that have to be reckoned with in this undertaking are so great that only the strongest faith in the power of the ethical spirit will let us venture on it.

First among them towers up the inability of our generation to understand what is and must be.

The men of the Renaissance and the Illuminati of the eighteenth century drew courage to desire the renewal of the world through ideas from their conviction of the absolute indefensibility of the material and spiritual conditions under which they lived. Unless with us, too, the many come to some such conviction, we must continue incapable of taking in hand this work, in which we must imitate them. But the many obstinately refuse to see things as they are, and hold with all their might to the most optimistic view of them that is possible. For this power, however, of idealizing with continually lowering ideals the reality which is felt to be ever less and less satisfying, pessimism also is partly responsible. Our generation, though so proud of its many achievements, no longer believes in the one thing which is all-essential: the spiritual advance of mankind. Having given up the expectation of this, it can put up with the present age without feeling such suffering as would compel it, for very pain, to long for a new one. What a task it will be to break the fetters of unthinking optimism and unthinking pessimism which hold us prisoners, and so to do what will pave the way for the renewal of civilization!

A second difficulty besetting the work which lies before us is that it is a piece of reconstruction. The ideas of civilization which our age needs are not new and strange to it. They have been in the possession of mankind already, and are to be found in many an antiquated formula. We have fundamentally nothing else to do than to restore to them the respect in which they were once held, and again regard them seriously as we bring them into relation with the reality which lies before us for treatment.

To make what is used up usable—is there a harder task ? " It is an impossible one," says history. "Never hitherto have worn-out ideas risen to new power among the peoples who have worn them out. Their disappearance has always been a final one."

That is true. In the history of civilization we find nothing but discouragement for our task. Anyone who finds history speaking optimistically lends her a language which is not her own.

Yet from the history of the past we can infer only what has been, not what will be. Even if it proves that no single people has ever lived through the decay of its civilization and a rebirth of it, we know at once that this, which has never happened yet, must happen with us, and therefore we cannot be content to say that the reasoned ethical ideas on which civilization rests get worn out in the course of history, and console ourselves with the reflection that this is exactly in accordance with the ordinary processes of nature. We require to know why it has so happened hitherto, and to draw an explanation, not from the analogy of nature, but from the laws of spiritual life. We want to get into our hands the key of the secret, so that we may with it unlock the new age, the age in which the worn out becomes again unworn and the spiritual and ethical can no longer get worn out. We must study the history of civilization otherwise than as our predecessors did, or we shall be finally lost.

Why do not thoughts which contribute to civilization retain the convincing power which they once had, and which they deserve on account of their content ? Why do they lose the evidential force of their moral and rational character ? Why do traditional truths cease to be realities and pass from mouth to mouth as mere phrases ?

*

*   *

Is this an unavoidable fate, or is the well drying up because our thinking did not go down to the permanent level of the water ?

Moreover, it is not merely that the past survives among us as something valueless ; it may cast a poisonous shade over us. There are thoughts on which we have never let our minds work directly because we found them ready formulated in history. Ideas which we have inherited do not let the truth which is in them come out into active service, but show it through a kind of dead mask. The worn-out achievements which pass over from a decadent civilization into the current of a new age often become like rejected products of metabolism, and act as poisons.

Granted that the Teutonic nations received a powerful stimulus to civilization at the Renaissance by reverting to the ideas of Greco-Roman thinkers, not less true is it that for many centuries they had been kept by that same Greco-Roman civilization in a condition of spiritual dependence which was wholly in contradiction to their native character. They took over from it decadent ideas which were for a long time a hindrance to their normal spiritual life, and thence came that strange mixture of strength and weakness which is the chief characteristic of the Middle Ages. The dangerous elements in the Greco-Roman civilization of the past still show themselves in our spiritual life. It is because Oriental and Greek conceptions which have had their day are still current among us that we bleed to death over problems which otherwise would have no existence for us. How much we suffer from the one fact that to-day and for several centuries past our thoughts about religion have been under the hereditary foreign domination of Jewish transcendentalism and Greek metaphysics, and, instead of

68

being able to express themselves naturally, have
suffered continual distortion !

Because ideas get worn out in this way, and in
this condition hinder the thinking of later generations, there is no continuity in the spiritual progress
of mankind, but only a confused succession of ups
and downs. The threads get broken, or knotted,
or lost, or when tied up again get tied wrongly.
Hitherto it has been thought possible to interpret
this up-and-down movement optimistically because
it was universally held that the Renaissance and
the age of the Illuminati were quite natural
successors of the Greco-Roman civilization, and it
was assumed further that, as a permanent result of
this, renewed civilizations would spring up in the
place of exhausted ones, and thus continual progress
be assured. But this generalization cannot justi-
fiably be drawn from such observations. It was
because new peoples came on the scene, who had
been only superficially touched by the decadent
civilizations and now produced others of their
own, that it was possible to see this succession of
ups and downs ending in an ascent. As a matter
of fact, however, our newer civilization was not
in any organic connection with the Greco-Roman,
even if it did take its first steps with the help of the
crutches which the latter provided ; it may be

described more truly as the reaction of a healthy spirit against the worn-out ideas which were thus offered to it. The essential element in the process was the contact of what was worn out with the fresh thought of young peoples.

To-day, however, all our thought is losing its power in its contact with the worn-out ideas of our expiring civilization, or—in the case of the Hindus and the Chinese—of our own and other expiring civilizations. The up-and-down movement will end, therefore, not in slow progress, but in unbroken descent—unless we can succeed in giving the worn-out ideas a renewal of their youth.

* \
* *

Another great difficulty in the way of the regeneration of our civilization lies in the fact that it must be an internal process, and not an external as well, and that, therefore, there is no place for healthy co-operation between the material and the spiritual. From the Renaissance to the middle of the nineteenth century the men who carried on the work of civilization could expect help towards spiritual progress from achievements in the sphere of external organization. Demands in each of these spheres stood side by side in their programme and were pushed on simultaneously. They were convinced that while working to trans-

form the institutions of public life they were
producing results which would call forth the
development of the new spiritual life. Success in
one sphere strengthened at once the hopes and the
energies that were at work in the other. They
laboured for the progressive democratization of the
State with the idea of thereby spreading through the
world the rule of grace and justice.

We, who have lived to see the spiritual bankruptcy of all the institutions which they created, can
no longer work in this way simultaneously at the
reform of institutions and the revival of the spiritual
element. The help which such co-operation would
give is denied us. We cannot even reckon any
longer on the old co-operation between knowledge
and thought. Once these two were allies. The
latter fought for freedom and in so doing made a
road for the former, and, on the other hand, all
the results attained by knowledge worked for the
general good of the spiritual life in that the reign
of law in nature was more and more clearly
demonstrated, and the reign of prejudice was
becoming continually more restricted. The alliance
also strengthened the thought that the well-being of
mankind must be based upon spiritual laws. Thus
knowledge and thought joined in establishing the
authority of reason and the rational tone of mind.

To-day thought gets no help from science, and the latter stands facing it independent and unconcerned. The newest scientific knowledge may be allied with an entirely unreflecting view of the universe. It maintains that it is concerned only with the establishment of individual facts, since it is only by means of these that scientific knowledge can maintain its practical character ; the co-ordination of the different branches of knowledge and the utilization of the results to form a theory of the universe are, it says, not its business. Once every man of science was also a thinker who counted for something in the general spiritual life of his generation. Our age has discovered how to divorce knowledge from thought, with the result that we have, indeed, a science which is free, but hardly any science left which reflects.

Thus we no longer have available for the renewal of our spiritual life any of the natural external helps which we used to have. We are called upon for a single kind of effort only, and have to work like men who are rebuilding the damaged foundations of a cathedral under the weight of the massive building. There is no progress in the world of phenomena to encourage us to persevere ; an immense revolution has to be brought about without the aid of any collateral revolutionary activities.

*

*   *

Again, the renewal of civilization is hindered by the fact that it is so exclusively the individual personality which must be looked to as the agent in the new movement.

The renewal of civilization has nothing to do with movements which bear the character of experiences of the crowd ; there are never anything but reactions to external happenings. But civilization can only revive when there shall come into being in a number of individuals a new tone of mind independent of the one prevalent among the crowd and in opposition to it, a tone of mind which will gradually win influence over the collective one, and in the end determine its character. It is only an ethical movement which can rescue us from the slough of barbarism, and the ethical comes into existence only in individuals.

The final decision as to what the future of a society shall be depends not on how near its organization is to perfection, but on the degrees of worthiness in its individual members. The most important, and yet the least easily determinable, element in history is the series of unobtrusive general changes which take place in the individual dispositions of the many. These are what precede and cause the happenings, and this is why it is so difficult to understand thoroughly the men and the events of past times. The character and worth of individuals among the mass and the way they work themselves into membership of the whole body, receiving influences from it and giving others back, we can even to-day only partially and uncertainly understand.

One thing, however, is clear. Where the collective body works more strongly on the individual than the latter does upon it, the result is deterioration, because the noble element on which everything depends, viz., the spiritual and moral worthiness of the individual, is thereby necessarily constricted and hampered. Decay of the spiritual and moral life then sets in, which renders society incapable of understanding and solving the problems which it has to face. Thereupon, sooner or later, it is involved in catastrophe.

That is the condition in which we are now, and that is why it is the duty of individuals to rise to a higher conception of their capabilities and undertake again the function which only the individual can perform, that of producing new spiritual-ethical ideas. If this does not come about in a multitude of cases nothing can save us.

A new public opinion must be created privately and unobtrusively. The existing one is maintained by the Press, by propaganda, by organization, and by financial and other influences which are at its disposal. This unnatural way of spreading ideas must be opposed by the natural one, which goes from man to man and relies solely on the truth of the thoughts and the hearer's receptiveness for new truth. Unarmed, and following the human spirit's primitive and natural fighting method, it must attack the other, which faces it, as Goliath faced David, in the mighty armour of the age.

About the struggle which must needs ensue no historical analogy can tell us much. The past has, no doubt, seen the struggle of the free-thinking individual against the fettered spirit of a whole society, but the problem has never presented itself on the scale on which it does to-day, because the fettering of the collective spirit as it is fettered to-day by modern organizations, modern unreflectiveness, and modern popular passions, is a phenomenon without precedent in history.

*

* *

Will the man of to-day have strength to carry out what the spirit demands from him, and what the age would like to make impossible ?

In the over-organized societies which in a hundred ways have him in their power, is he destined to become once more an independent personality and to exert influence back upon them? They will use every means to keep him in that condition of impersonality which suits them. They fear personality because the spirit and the truth, which they would like to muzzle, find in it a means of expressing themselves. And their power is, unfortunately, as great as their fear.

There is a tragic alliance between society as a whole and its economic conditions. With a grim relentlessness those conditions tend to bring up the man of to-day as a being without freedom, without self-collectedness, without independence, in short as a human being so full of deficiencies that he lacks the qualities of humanity. And they are the last things that we can change. Even if it should be granted us that the spirit should begin its work, we shall only slowly and incompletely gain power over these forces. There is, in fact, being demanded from the will that which our conditions of life refuse to allow.

And how heavy the tasks that the spirit has to take in hand! It has to create the power of understanding the truth that is really true where at present nothing is current but propagandist truth. It has to depose ignoble patriotism, and enthrone the noble kind of patriotism which aims at ends that are worthy of the whole of mankind, in circles where the hopeless issues of past and present

political activities keep nationalist passions aglow
even among those who in their hearts would fain be
free from them. It has to get the fact that civilization is an interest of all men and of humanity as a
whole recognized again in places where national
civilization is to-day worshipped as an idol, and
the notion of a humanity with a common civilization lies broken to fragments. It has to maintain
our faith in the civilized State, even though our
modern States, spiritually and economically ruined
by the war, have no time to think about the
tasks of civilization, and dare not devote their
attention to anything but how to use every
possible means, even those which undermine the
conception of justice, to collect money with which
to prolong their own existence. It has to unite
us by giving us a single ideal of civilized man,
and this in a world where one nation has robbed
its neighbour of all faith in humanity, idealism,
righteousness, reasonableness, and truthfulness, and
all alike have come under the domination of powers
which are plunging us ever deeper into barbarism.
It has to get attention concentrated on civilization
while the growing difficulty of making a living
absorbs the masses more and more in material cares,
and makes all other things seem to them to be mere
shadows. It has to give us faith in the possibility of

progress while the reaction of the economic on the spiritual becomes more pernicious every day and contributes to an ever growing demoralization. It has to provide us with a capacity for hope at a time when not only secular and religious institutions and associations, but the men, too, who are looked upon as leaders, continually fail us, when artists and men of learning show themselves as supporters of barbarism, and notabilities who pass for thinkers, and behave outwardly as such, are revealed, when crises come, as being nothing more than writers and members of academies.

All these hindrances stand in the path of the will to civilization. A dull despair hovers about us. How well we now understand the men of the Greco-Roman decadence, who stood before events incapable of resistance, and, leaving the world to its fate, withdrew upon their inner selves ! Like them, we are bewildered by our experience of life. Like them, we hear enticing voices which say to us that the one thing which can still make life tolerable is to live for the day. We must, we are told, renounce every wish to think or hope about anything beyond our own fate. We must find rest in resignation.

The recognition that civilization is founded on some sort of theory of the universe, and can be restored only through a spiritual awakening and a will for ethical good in the mass of mankind, compels us to make clear to ourselves those difficulties in the way of a rebirth of civilization which ordinary reflection would overlook. But at the same time it raises us above all considerations of possibility or impossibility. If the ethical spirit provides a sufficient standing ground in the sphere of events for making civilization a reality, then we shall get civilization, provided that we return to a suitable theory of the universe and the convictions to which this properly gives birth.

The history of our decadence preaches the truth that when hope is dead the spirit becomes the deciding court of appeal, and this truth will in the future find in us a sublime and noble fulfilment.

CHAPTER V

CIVILIZATION AND THEORIES OF THE UNIVERSE

The regeneration of our theory of the universe and the restoration of civilization. A reflective theory of the universe; rationalism and mysticism. The optimistic-ethical theory as a theory of civilization. The regeneration of our ideas by reflection about the meaning of life.

THE greatest of all the spirit's tasks is to produce a theory of the universe (*Weltanschauung**), for in such a theory all the ideas, convictions and activities of an age have their roots, and it is only when we have arrived at one which is compatible with civilization that we are capable of holding the ideas and convictions which are the conditions of civilization in general.

What is meant by a theory of the universe ? It is the content of the thoughts of society and the individuals which compose it about the nature and object of the world in which they live, and the position and the destiny of mankind and of individual men within it. What significance have the society in which I live and I myself in the world ? What do we want to do in the world, what do we

* Translated "world-view" throughout the second part of these Lectures.

hope to get from it, and what is our duty to it ?
The answer given by the majority to these fundamental questions about existence decides what the
spirit is in which they and their age live.

Is not this putting too high the value of a theory
of the universe ?

At present, certainly, the majority do not, as a
rule, attain to any properly thought-out theory, nor
do they feel the need of deriving their ideas and
convictions from such a source. They are in tune,
more or less, with all the tones which pervade the
age in which they live.

But who are the musicians who have produced
these tones ? They are the personalities who have
thought out theories of the universe, and drawn
from them the ideas, more or less valuable, which
are current amongst us to-day. In this way all
thoughts, whether those of individuals or those of
society, go back ultimately, in some way or other,
to a theory of the universe. Every age lives in the
consciousness of what has been provided for it by
the thinkers under whose influence it stands.

Plato was wrong in holding that the philosophers
of a State should also be its governors. Their
supremacy is a different and a higher one than that
which consists in taking cognizance of laws and
ordinances and giving effect to official authority.

They are the officers of the general staff who sit in the background thinking out, with more or less clearness of vision, the details of the battle which is to be fought. Those who play their part in the public eye are the subordinate officers who, for their variously sized units, convert the general directions of the staff into orders of the day: namely, that the forces will start at such and such a time, move in this or that direction, and occupy this or that point. Kant and Hegel have commanded millions who had never read a line of their writings, and who did not even know that they were obeying their orders.

Those who command, whether it be in a large or a small sphere, can only carry out what is already in the thought of the age. They do not build the instrument on which they have to play, but are merely given a seat at it. Nor do they compose the piece they have to play; it is simply put before them, and they cannot alter it; they can only reproduce it with more or less skill and success. If it is meaningless, they cannot do much to improve it, but neither, if it is good, can they damage it seriously.

To the question, then, whether it is personalities or ideas which decide the fate of an age, the answer is that the age gets its ideas from personalities. If the thinkers of a certain period produce a worthy theory of the universe, then ideas pass into cur-

rency which guarantee progress; if they are not
capable of such production, then decadence sets in
in some form or other.   Every theory of the universe
draws after it its own special results in history.

The fall of the Roman Empire in spite of that
empire's having over it so many rulers of con-
spicuous ability, may be traced ultimately to the
fact that ancient philosophy produced no theory of
the universe with ideas which tended to that
empire's preservation.   With the rise of Stoicism,
as the definitive answer of the philosophic thought
of antiquity, the fate of the world down to the
Middle Ages was decided.   The idea of resignation,
noble idea as it is, could not ensure progress in a
world-wide empire.   The efforts of its strongest
emperors were useless.   The yarn with which they
had to weave was rotten.

In the eighteenth century, under the rule, in most
places, of insignificant rococo-sovereigns and rococo-
ministers, a progressive movement began among
the nations of Europe which was unique in the
history of the world.   Why ?   The thinkers of the
Illuminati and of rationalism produced a worthy
theory of the universe from which worthy ideas
were spread among mankind.

But when history began to shape itself in accordance with these ideas, the thought which had

produced the progress came to a halt, and we have
now a generation which is squandering the precious
heritage it has received from the past, and is living
in a world of ruins, because it cannot complete the
building which that past began. Even had our
rulers and statesmen been less short-sighted than
they actually were, they would not in the long run
have been able to avert the catastrophe which
burst upon us. Both the inner and the outer
collapse of civilization were latent in the circumstances produced by the prevalent view of the
universe. The rulers, small and great alike, did not
act in accordance with the spirit of the age.

With the disappearance of the influence exerted
by the *Aufklärung*, rationalism, and the serious
philosophy of the early nineteenth century, the seeds
were sown of the world-war to come. Then began
to disappear also the ideas and convictions which
would have made possible a solution on right lines
of the controversies which arise between nations.

Thus the course of events brought us into a
position in which we had to get along without any
real theory of the universe. The collapse of
philosophy and the rise and influence of scientific
modes of thought made it impossible to arrive at
an idealist theory which should satisfy thought.
Moreover, our age is poorer in deep thinkers than
perhaps any preceding one. There were a few

strong spirits who, with varied knowledge and with
devoted efforts, offered the world some patchwork
thought ; there were some dazzling comets ; but
that was all that was granted us. Their products
in the way of world theories were good enough to
interest a circle of academic culture, or to delight a
few believing followers, but the people as a whole
were entirely untouched.

We began, therefore, to persuade ourselves that
it was, after all, possible to get through without any
theory of the universe. The feeling that we needed
to stir ourselves up to ask questions about the world
and life, and to come to a decision upon them,
gradually died away. In the unreflective condition
to which we had surrendered ourselves, we took, to
meet the claims of our own life and the nation's life,
the chance ideas provided by our feeling for reality.
During more than a generation and a half we
had proof enough and to spare that the theory
which is the result of absence of theory is the most
worthless of all, involving not only ruin to the
spiritual life, but ruin universal. For where there
is no general staff to think out its plan of campaign
for any generation its subordinate officers lead it,
as in actual warfare so in the sphere of ideas, from
one profitless adventure to another.

The reconstruction of our age, then, can begin

only with a reconstruction of a theory of the universe. There is hardly anything more urgent in its claim on us than this which seems to be so far off and abstract. Only when we have made ourselves at home again in the solid thought-building of a theory which can support a civilization, and when we take from it, all of us in co-operation, ideas which can stimulate our life and work, only then can there again arise a society which shall possess ideals with magnificent aims and be able to bring these into effective agreement with reality. It is from new ideas that we must build history anew.

For individuals as for the community, life without a theory of things is a pathological disturbance of the higher capacity for self-direction.

*

*　　　　　*

What conditions must a theory of the universe fulfil to enable it to create a civilization ?

First, and defined generally, it must be the product of thought. Nothing but what is born of thought and addresses itself to thought can be a spiritual power affecting the whole of mankind. Only what has been well turned over in the thought of the many, and thus recognized as truth, possesses a natural power of conviction which will work on other minds and will continue to be effective. Only where there is a constant appeal to the need

of a reflective view of things are all man's spiritual
capacities called into activity.

Our age has a kind of artistic prejudice against a
reflective theory of the universe. We are still
children of the Romantic movement to a greater
extent than we realize. What that movement
produced in opposition to the *Aufklärung* and to
rationalism seems to us valid for all ages against
any theory that would found itself solely on thought.
In such a theory of the universe we can see before-
hand the world dominated by a barren intellectualism, convictions governed by mere utility, and
a shallow optimism, which together throw a wet
blanket over all human genius and enthusiasm.

In a great deal of the opposition which it offered
to rationalism the reaction of the early nineteenth
century was right. Nevertheless it remains true
that it despised and distorted what was, in spite of
all its imperfections, the greatest and most valuable
manifestation of the spiritual life of man that the
world has yet seen. Down through all circles of
cultured and uncultured alike there prevailed at
that time a belief in thought and a reverence for
truth. For that reason alone that age stands
higher than any which preceded it, and much
higher than our own.

At no price must the feelings and phrases of

Romanticism be allowed to prevent our generation from forming a clear conception of what reason really is. It is no dry intellectualism which would suppress all the manifold movements of our inner life, but the totality of all the functions of our spirit in their living action and interaction. In it our intellect and our will hold that mysterious intercourse which determines the character of our spiritual being. These fundamental ideas which it produces contain all that we can feel or imagine about our destiny and that of mankind, and give our whole being its direction and its value. The enthusiasm which comes from thought has the same relation to that which rises from the cauldron of feeling as the wind which sweeps the heights has to that which eddies about between the hills. If we venture once more to seek help from the light of reason, we shall no longer keep ourselves down at the level of a generation which has ceased to be capable of enthusiasm, but shall follow the deep and noble passion inspired by great and sublime ideals. This will so fill and expand our being that that by which we now live will seem to be merely a petty kind of excitement, and will disappear.

Rationalism is more than a movement of thought which realized itself at the end of the eighteenth and the beginning of the nineteenth centuries. It is a necessary phenomenon in all normal spiritual life.

All real progress in the world is in the last analysis produced by rationalism.

It is true that the intellectual productions of the period which we designate historically as the rationalistic are incomplete and unsatisfactory, but the principle, which was then established, of basing our views of the universe on thought and thought alone, is valid for all time. Even if the tree's earliest fruit did not ripen perfectly, the tree itself remains, nevertheless, the tree of life for the life of our spirit.

All the movements that have claimed to take the place of rationalism stand far below it in the matter of achievement. From speculative thought, from history, from feeling, from æsthetics, from science, they tried to construct a theory of the universe, grubbing at haphazard in the world around them instead of excavating scientifically. Rationalism alone chose the right place for its digging, and dug systematically, according to plan. If it found only metal of small value, that was because, with the means at its disposal, it could not go deep enough. Impoverished and ruined as we are because we sought as mere adventurers, we must make up our minds to sink another shaft in the ground where rationalism worked, and to go down through all the strata to see whether we cannot find the gold which must certainly be there.

To think out to the end a theory of the universe which has been produced by thought—that is the only possible way of finding our bearings amid the confusion of the world of thought to-day.

Philosophical, historical, and scientific questions with which it was not capable of dealing overwhelmed the earlier rationalism like an avalanche, and buried it in the middle of its journey. The new rational theory of the universe must work its way out of this chaos. Leaving itself freely open to the whole influence of the world of fact, it must explore every path offered by reflection and knowledge in its effort to reach the ultimate meaning of being and life, and to see whether it can solve some of the riddles which they present.

The ultimate knowledge, in which man recognizes his own being as a part of the All, belongs, they say, to the realm of mysticism, by which is meant that he does not reach it by the method of ordinary reflection, but somehow or other lives himself into it.

But why assume that the road of thought must suddenly stop at the frontier of mysticism ? It is true that pure reason has hitherto called a halt whenever it came into this neighbourhood, for it was unwilling to go beyond the point at which it could still exhibit everything as part of a smooth, logical plan. Mysticism, on its side, always depre-

ciated pure reason as much as it could, to prevent
at all costs the idea from gaining currency that it
was in any way bound to give an account to reason.
And yet, although they refuse to recognize each
other, the two belong to each other.

It is in reason that intellect and will, which in our
nature are mysteriously bound up together, seek
to come to a mutual understanding. The ultimate
knowledge that we strive to acquire is knowledge of
life, which intellect looks at from without, will from
within. Since life is the ultimate object of knowledge, our ultimate knowledge is necessarily our
thinking experience of life, but this does not lie
outside the sphere of reason, but within reason itself.
Only when the will has thought out its relation to
the intellect, has come, as far as it can, into line
with it, has penetrated it, and in it become logical,
is it in a position to comprehend itself, so far as its
nature allows this, as a part of the universal will-to-
live and a part of being in general. If it merely
leaves the intellect on one side, it loses itself in
confused imaginings, while the intellect, which, like
the rationalism of the past, will not allow that in
order to understand life it must finally lose itself in
thinking experience, renounces all hope of con-
structing a deep and firmly based theory of the
universe.

Thus reflection, when pursued to the end, leads somewhere and somehow to a living mysticism, which is for all men everywhere a necessary element of thought.

Doubts whether the mass of men can ever attain to that level of reflection about themselves and the world which is demanded by a reflective theory of the universe, are quite justifiable if the man of to-day is taken as an example of the race. But he, with his diminished need of thought, is a pathological phenomenon.

In reality there is given in the mental endowment of the average man a capacity for thought which to the individual makes the creation of a reflective theory of things of his own not only possible, but under normal conditions even a necessity. The great movements of illumination in ancient and modern times help to maintain the confident belief that there is in the mass of mankind a power of thought on fundamentals which can be roused to activity. This belief is strengthened by observation of mankind and intercourse with the young. A fundamental impulse to reflect about the universe stirs us during those years in which we begin to think independently. Later on we let it languish, even though feeling clearly that we thereby impoverish ourselves and become less capable of what is good. We are like springs of water which no longer run because they have not been watched and have gradually become choked with rubbish.

More than any other age has our own neglected to watch the thousand springs of thought ; hence the drought in which we are pining. But if we only go on to remove the rubbish which conceals the water, the sands will be irrigated again, and life will spring up where hitherto there has been only a desert.

Certainly there are guides and the guided in the department of world-theories, as in others. So far the independence of the mass of men remains a relative one. The question is only whether the influence of the guides leads to dependence or independence. The latter brings with it a development in the direction of truthfulness ; the former means the death of that virtue.

Every being who calls himself a man is meant to develop into a real personality within a reflective theory of the universe which he has created for himself.

*

* *

But of what character must the theory be if ideas and convictions about civilization are to be based on it ?

That theory of the universe is optimistic which

gives existence the preference as against non-existence and thus affirms life as something possessing value in itself. From this attitude to the universe and to life results the impulse to raise existence, in so far as our influence can affect it, to its highest level of value. Thence originates activity directed to the improvement of the living conditions of individuals, of society, of nations and of humanity, from which spring the external achievements of civilization, the lordship of spirit over the powers of nature, and the higher social organization.

Ethics is the activity of man directed to secure the inner perfection of his own personality. In itself it is quite independent of whether the theory of the universe is pessimistic or optimistic. But its sphere of action is contracted or widened according as it appears in connection with a theory of the first or the second type.

In the determinist-pessimistic theory of the universe, as we have it in the thought of the Brāhmans or of Schopenhauer, ethics has nothing whatever to do with the objective world. It aims solely at securing the self-perfection of the individual as this comes to pass in inner freedom and disconnection from the world and the spirit of the world.

But the scope of ethics is extended in proportion

as it develops and strengthens a connection with a theory of the universe which is affirmative toward the world and life. Its aim is now the inner perfection of the individual and at the same time the direction of his activity so as to take effect on other men and on the objective world. It is true that in face of the objective world and its spirit ethics no longer holds itself up to man as an aim in itself. By its means man is to become capable of acting among men and in the world as a higher and purer force, and thus to do his part towards the actualization of the ideal of general progress.

Thus the optimistic-ethical theory of the universe works in partnership with ethics to produce civilization. Neither is capable of doing so by itself. Optimism supplies confidence that the world-process has somehow or other a spiritual-sensible aim, and that the improvement of the general relations of the world and of society promotes the spiritual-moral perfection of the individual. From ethics is derived ability to develop the purposive state of mind necessary to produce action on the world and society and to cause the co-operation of all our achievements to secure the spiritual and moral perfection of the individual which is the final end of civilization.

Once we have recognized that the energies which spring out of a theory of the universe, and impel us to create a civilization, are rooted in the ethical and the optimistic, we get light on the question why and how our ideals of civilization got worn out. This question is not to be answered by good or bad analogies from nature. The decisive answer is that they got worn out because we had not succeeded in establishing the ethical and optimistic elements on a sufficiently firm foundation.

If we should analyse the process in which the ideas and convictions that produce civilization reveal themselves, it would be found that whenever an advance has been registered, either the optimist or the ethical element in the theory of the universe has proved more attractive than usual, and has had as its consequence a progressive development. When civilization is decaying there is the same chain of causation, but it works negatively. The building is damaged or falls in because the optimist element or the ethical, or both, give way like a weak foundation. No amount of inquiry will give any other reason for the changes. All imaginable ideas and convictions of that character spring from optimism and the ethical impulse. If these two pillars are strong enough, we need have no fears about the building.

The future of civilization depends, therefore, on whether it is possible for thought to reach a theory of the universe which will have a more secure and

fundamental hold on optimism and the ethical
impulse than its predecessors have had.

*

*   *

We Westerners dream of a theory of the
universe which corresponds to our impulse to
action and at the same time justifies it. We
have not been able to formulate such a theory
definitely. At present we are in the state of possessing merely an impulse without any definite orientation. The spirit of the age drives us into action
without allowing us to attain any clear view of the
objective world and of life. It claims our toil
inexorably in the service of this or that end, this or
that achievement. It keeps us in a sort of intoxi-
cation of activity so that we may never have time
to reflect and to ask ourselves what this restless
sacrifice of ourselves to ends and achievements really
has to do with the meaning of the world and of our
lives. And so we wander hither and thither in the
gathering dusk formed by lack of any definite theory
of the universe like homeless, drunken mercenaries,
and enlist indifferently in the service of the common
and the great without distinguishing between them.
And the more hopeless becomes the condition of the
world in which this adventurous impulse to action
and progress ranges to and fro, the more bewildered

becomes our whole conception of things and the more purposeless and irrational the doings of those who have enlisted under the banner of such an impulse.

How little reflection is present in the Western impulse to action becomes evident when this tries to square its ideas with those of the Far East. For thought in the Far East has been constantly occupied in its search for the meaning of life, and forces us to consider the problem of the meaning of our own restlessness, the problem which we Westerners burke so persistently. We are utterly at a loss when we contemplate the ideas which are presented to us in Indian thought. We turn away from the intellectual presumption which we find there. We are conscious of the unsatisfying and incomplete elements in the ideal of cessation from action. We feel instinctively that the will-to-progress is justified not only in its aspect as directed to the spiritual perfection of personality, but also in that which looks towards the general and material.

For ourselves we dare to allege that we adventurers, who take up an affirmative attitude toward the world and toward life, however great and even ghastly our mistakes may be, can yet show not only greater material, but also greater spiritual and ethical, contributions than can those who lie under the ban of a theory of the universe characterized by cessation from action.

And yet, all the same, we cannot feel ourselves completely justified in the face of these strange Eastern theories. They have in them something full of nobility which retains its hold on us, even fascinates us. This tinge of nobility comes from the fact that these convictions are born of a search for a theory of the universe and for the meaning of life. With us, on the other hand, activist instincts and impulses take the place of a theory of the universe. We have no theory affirming the world and life to oppose to the negative theory of these thinkers, no thought which has found a basis for an optimistic conception of existence to oppose to this other, which has arrived at a pessimistic conception.

The reawakening of the Western spirit must thus begin by our people, educated and simple alike, becoming conscious of their lack of a theory of the universe and feeling the horror of their consequent position. We can no longer be satisfied to make shift with substitutes for such a theory. What is the basis of the will-to-activity and progress which impels both to great actions and to terrible deeds, and which tries to keep us from reflection ? We must bend all our energies to the solution of this problem.

There is only one way in which we can hope to emerge from the meaningless state in which we are now held captive into one informed with meaning. Each one of us must turn to contemplate his own being, and we must all give ourselves to co-operative reflection so as to discover how our will to action and to progress may be intellectually based on the way in which we interpret our own lives and the life around us, and the meaning which we give to these.

The great revision of the convictions and ideals in which and for which we live will only take place when, by constantly proclaiming them, we have given currency among our contemporaries to ideas and thoughts other and better than those by which they are dominated at the moment. Only thus will the many come to reflect about the meaning of life and to reorientate, revise and make over again their ideals of action and of progress, asking themselves whether these have a meaning in accord with that which we attribute to our life itself. This personal reflection about final and elemental things is the one and only reliable way of measuring values. My willing and doing have real meaning and value only in proportion as the aims which action sets before itself can be justified as being in direct accord with my interpretation of my own and of other life. All else, however much it may pass current as approved by tradition, usage, and public opinion, is vain and dangerous.

It seems, indeed, a matter for scorn and derision

that we should urge men to anything so remote as
a return to reflection about the meaning of life at a
time when the sufferings and the follies of the
nations have become so intense and so extended,
when unemployment and poverty and starvation
are rife, when power is being dissipated on all sides
in the most shameless and senseless way, and when
organized human life is dislocated in every direction.
But only when the general population begins to
reflect in this way will forces come into being which
will be able to effect something to counterbalance
all this ruin and misery. Whatever other measures
it is attempted to carry out will have doubtful and
altogether inadequate results.

When in the spring the withered grey of the
pastures gives place to green, this is due to the
millions of young shoots which sprout up freshly
from the old roots. In like manner the revival of
thought which is essential for our time can only
come through a transformation of the opinions and
ideals of the many brought about by individual and
universal reflection about the meaning of life and of
the world.

But are we sure of being able to think out that
affirmation of the world and of life, which is such
a powerful impulse in us, into a theory of the world
and of life from which a stream of energy productive

of intelligible life and action may convincingly and
constantly proceed? How are we to succeed in
doing what the spirit of the Western world during
past generations has in vain toiled to accomplish?

Even if thought, once more awakened, should only
attain to an incomplete and unsatisfying theory of
the universe, yet this, as the truth to which we have
ourselves worked through, would be of more value
than a complete lack of any theory at all, or, alter-
natively, than any sort of authoritative theory to
which, neglecting the demands of true thought, we
cling on account of its supposed intrinsic value
without having any real and thorough belief in it.

The beginning of all spiritual life of any real value
is courageous faith in truth and open confession of
the same. The most profound religious experience,
too, is not alien to thought, but must be capable of
derivation from this if it is to be given a true and
deep basis. Mere reflection about the meaning of
life has already value in itself. If such reflection
should again come into being amongst us, the ideals,
born of vanity and of suffering, which now flourish
in rank profusion like evil weeds among the convictions of the generality of people, would infallibly
wither away and die. How much would already be
accomplished towards our salvation from our present
circumstances if only we would all give up three
minutes every evening to gazing up into the infinite

world of the starry heavens and meditating on it,
or if in taking part in a funeral procession we would
reflect on the enigma of life and death, instead of
engaging in thoughtless conversation as we follow
behind the coffin! The ideals, born of folly and
suffering, of those who make public opinion and
direct public events, would have no more power over
men if they once began to reflect about eternity and
mortality, existence and dissolution, and thus learnt
to distinguish between true and false standards,
between those which possess real value and those
which do not. The old-time rabbis used to teach
that the kingdom of God would come if only the
whole of Israel would really keep a single Sabbath
simultaneously! How much more is it true that
the injustice and violence and untruth, which are
now bringing so much disaster on the human race,
would lose their power if only a single real trace of
reflection about the meaning of the world and of life
should appear amongst us!

But is there not a danger in challenging men with
this question about the meaning of life and in
demanding that our impulse to action should justify
and clarify itself in such reflection as that of which
we have spoken? Shall we not lose, in acceding to
this demand, some irreplaceable element of naïve
enthusiasm?

We need not thus be anxious as to how strong or how weak our impulse to action will prove to be when it shall have arrived, as the result of intellectual reflection, at an interpretation of life. Only that has real meaning for life which is given as an element of our interpretation of life. It is not the quantity, but the quality, of activity that really matters. What is needed is that our will-to-action should become conscious of itself and should cease to work blindly.

But perhaps, it may be objected, we shall end in the resignation of agnosticism, and shall be obliged to confess that we cannot discover any meaning in the universe or in life.

If thought is to set out on its journey unhampered, it must be prepared for anything, even for arrival at intellectual agnosticism. But even if our will-to-action is destined to wrestle endlessly and unavailingly with an agnostic view of the universe and of life, still this painful disenchantment is better for it than persistent refusal to think out its position at all. For this disenchantment does, at any rate, mean that we are clear as to what we are doing.

There is, however, no necessity whatever for such an attitude of resignation. We feel that a position of affirmation regarding the world and life is something which is in itself both necessary and valuable. Therefore it is at least likely that a foundation can be

found for it in thought. Since it is an innate
element of our will-to-live, it must be possible to
comprehend it as a necessary corollary to our interpretation of life. Perhaps we shall have to look
elsewhere than we have done hitherto for the real
basis of that theory of the universe which carries
with it affirmation of the world and of life. Previous
thought imagined that it could deduce the meaning
of life from its interpretation of the universe. It
may be that we shall be obliged to resign ourselves
to abandon the problem of the interpretation of the
universe and to find the meaning of our life in the
will-to-live as this exists in ourselves.

The ways along which we have to struggle toward
the goal may be veiled in darkness, yet the direction
in which we must travel is clear. We must reflect
together about the meaning of life; we must strive
together to attain to a theory of the universe
affirmative of the world and of life, in which the
impulse to action which we experience as a necessary
and valuable element of our being may find justification, orientation, clarity and depth, may receive a
fresh access of moral strength, and be retempered,
and thus become capable of formulating, and of
acting on, definite ideals of civilization, inspired by
the spirit of true humanitarianism.